SHARE

For Sachin, who SHARES life with me

SHARE

Asian-inspired plates to impress your guests

NISHA PARMAR

Photography by Nassima Rothacker

Hardie Grant

QUADRILLE

Managing Director Sarah Lavelle
Senior Commissioning Editor Sophie Allen
Design and Art Direction Gemma Hayden
Photographer Nassima Rothacker
Photographer's Assistants Kee Kunnath & Amy Grover
Food Stylist Amy Stephenson
Food Stylist's Assistants Sophie Pryn, Valeria Russo & Hattie Baker
Prop Stylist Faye Wears
Production Director Stephen Lang
Production Controller Katie Jarvis

Published in 2023 by Quadrille,
an imprint of Hardie Grant Publishing

Quadrille
52–54 Southwark Street
London SE1 1UN

quadrille.com

Text © Nisha Parmar 2023
Photography © Nassima Rothacker 2023
Design © Quadrille 2023

ISBN 9781837830237
Printed with soy inks in China

contents

introduction

*'It seems such a privilege now, the idea of being
able to cook for other people, and not because we
have to, but because we want to.'*
– Nigella Lawson

food tastes better shared

My sister would call me in a frenzy: 'I'm having guests over for dinner tomorrow, what should I cook? Give me some ideas, I want to impress them but nothing too complicated!'

For me, this is the ultimate challenge. I adore the process of creating a menu, shopping for ingredients, and producing a gorgeous yet effortless meal for others to savour. It's what fills my heart with joy, but often overwhelms others with anxiety.

My life took an unexpected turn when I landed my dream job of cooking dinner parties professionally. I had spent 17 years in the corporate banking world when my husband encouraged me to apply for MasterChef UK. I never imagined it would lead to the career change I had longed for but I finally discovered my purpose in life – to nourish others.

When I was growing up, my mother frequently hosted dinner parties for no apparent reason – whether there was something or nothing to celebrate, feeding others was a quintessential Indian tradition. Sharing food was our simple yet sincere way of expressing emotions. As guests arrived at our home, they were treated with great hospitality. I vividly recall my mother's attention to detail, using her best china, finest tablecloth, and occasionally even sharing her hidden stash of Ferrero Rocher chocolates that were reserved for 'guests only'! Food has been the social glue of Indian families, a universal language of love. We weren't a family that hugged or expressed 'I love you' frequently. Instead, we demonstrated our affection by preparing large pots of biryani or other beloved dishes.

Food has the power to unite people, nourish their body, mind and soul. It evokes emotions and nostalgia, often best shared with loved ones.

For me, cooking food for others is a ceremonious art. Whether it's a pot of curry served buffet-style or an elegantly plated dish one would typically order at a restaurant, the end result is everything – seeing joyful expressions on people's faces. A delicious meal can truly make a bad day better and lift spirits during challenging times.

However, times have changed. Time is scarce, and expenses have risen. We need to entertain without breaking the bank, and I've been mindful of these aspects in this book.

As you weave your way through these pages, I hope the recipes inspire you to host your own dinner party and experience the same elation I feel when cooking for others. It's uplifting and addictive – nothing compares to a meal prepared with love.

from school dinners to MasterChef

It might seem overly dramatic, especially since I didn't win the competition, but MasterChef had a tremendous impact on my life. My love for food had begun in an unusual setting: the school dinner hall queue was my favourite time of day. While my mother prepared delicious Indian dishes at home, my first experience of non-Indian cuisine, such as roast chicken, bangers and mash and spaghetti bolognese, was at school. I loved it! I tried to convince my mother to make pasta for dinner, but she had no idea what it was, so she served me curried pasta with chapati, which was a carbohydrate overdose! This experience led me to realize that I wanted more variety in my food, and to learn to cook dishes from other cultures.

As a child, I had basic cooking skills, as my mother had me preparing salads when I was just six years old. It was like a kitchen hierarchy, and as you progressed from the salad counter, you would learn to spread butter on chapati, make the dough, and eventually roll it out. Although I enjoyed learning Indian cooking techniques, I also longed to learn about other cuisines. I didn't want to eat curry, rice, chapati or daal every day. I was proud of my Indian heritage and at the same time felt connected to my British upbringing. After school, I watched shows like Blue Peter and Ready Steady Cook and imagined myself cooking on television.

At the age of ten, my famous dish was a vegetable lasagne, which my mother bragged about to our family members and even used as bait to entice them to visit us. It was exhilarating to create food that tasted good and was worthy of serving to others. As a teenager, I discovered the joys of eating out, and travelling, which introduced me to a world of new cuisines. At university, my flatmate was studying food science, and I found myself more interested in her course than my own economics degree. However, pursuing a career in cooking was not acceptable in my culture, so I didn't consider my hobby a viable career option and kept it to myself.

from banker to chef's whites

I never realized I had a 'talent'. I thought everyone cooked, until people said to me:

'You have flavour oozing from your fingertips.' Gregg Wallace

'That is a gastronomic triumph, Nisha.' Amol Rajan

'You've just cooked a restaurant-worthy dish and most chefs can't cook fish that well.' Nathan Outlaw

'Boom! That is so new, refreshing and clever.' John Torode

During my time on MasterChef, I found it difficult to accept praise like this and often appeared shocked by it. Although I didn't emerge as the winner, looking back I believe it was a blessing not to have won. It allowed me to take in the advice and grow in confidence with my cooking. With no pressure or expectation from the public, I was able to quietly reflect on how to use my newfound knowledge of cooking.

Gregg Wallace described me as *'the most successful non-winner MasterChef has had'*.

I mean, coming from the judge, this is everything, and a powerful message that in life you don't have to win to be a winner.

After I left MasterChef, I went back to work the next day like nothing ever happened. Holding this big secret inside, I pretended I had been off on study leave for financial exams! As I sat at my desk staring at spreadsheets, I felt my soul slowly withering away. Although my work was familiar and had been my routine for the past 17 years, I felt lost. It dawned on me that my true calling was cooking, and it was the thing that brought me genuine happiness. However, I faced a dilemma: how could I pursue my passion while balancing my well-paid job, mortgage and responsibilities as a parent? I couldn't simply abandon everything for a pipe dream, especially since I had no other job lined up in the culinary industry. I lacked a concrete plan.

And just like that, my colleague turned around and asked: 'Nisha, are you free next Saturday? I need a dinner party cooked for some friends at my house; can you do it?' I immediately said yes, absolutely 100 percent, that sounds wonderful. Then afterwards I freaked out. I had no idea how to host a dinner party for 16 people! How do I prepare and transport it; what will I cook? Fast forward and somehow I managed, with the help of some friends I met on MasterChef, to create a five-course dinner party – and it was a huge success! I posted a few photos on Instagram and suddenly everyone wanted to book my dinner-party experience. Without knowing it, I had organically created a business model that I didn't know existed! Most chefs go down the restaurant route, but with my two young sons, I didn't want to give up my evenings with them. So, I found a way to do what I love and still be there for my family. And that is how Nisha's Dinner Party was born!

I was living a double life – banking it up Monday to Friday and cooking up a storm nearly every other weekend in people's homes. It was a non-stop juggling act that left me feeling drained and exhausted. After a year of being fully booked with dinner parties, I knew I couldn't keep up this crazy pace forever. So I made the big, bold and brave decision to leave my job. It was a scary move, but also super exciting. I realized it was now or never, and I couldn't let fear hold me back any longer. It turned out to be the best decision I ever made!

As I walked out of those Canary Wharf towers for the very last time, I felt a deep sense of freedom and fear in equal measure. The fear of failing kept me motivated to work as hard as ever.

The opportunities started to flood in, and suddenly I was busier than ever before – but I loved every single moment of it! And then, just when I thought things couldn't get any better, my food adventure was catapulted to the next level by one person. It all started when I had the privilege of designing the dinner menu for the Soccer Aid Gala in 2019 at The Science Museum in London, thanks to a recommendation from the director of Unicef, who I had looked after at the bank. As I was busy in the kitchen, one of the waiters approached me and said that Table 21 wanted to speak with the chef. And to my surprise, it was none other than Joe Wicks! My heart raced with nervous energy, wondering what could be wrong with the food. But to my relief, Joe gushed that the food was amazing and asked where my restaurant was located. I explained that I only did dinner parties in the comfort of the client's home.

After booking me, it took six weeks before I found myself cooking a seven-course menu at Joe's home for him and his circle of family and friends. At that point, I wasn't well-versed in using Instagram, while Joe was already a social media sensation. He posted a few videos of our dinner party, which caused my Instagram account to explode – my follower count skyrocketed from 5,000 to 20,000 within 24 hours. This sudden surge of attention was overwhelming, and it took me a few days to fully grasp the enormity of what had just happened.

Over time, Joe and I have become great friends, and I've cooked for him several times, got to know his entire family and watched his children grow up. Joe has become my mentor, and I'm inspired by his humble and hard-working attitude.

Cooking for celebrities kickstarted my career. As I catered their high-profile dinner parties, I realized how much they appreciated the privacy I provided. But more than that, they were blown away by the food I served, and the word-of-mouth recommendations started.

With my celebrity clientele increasing, I struggled to take on all the bookings. So, in the autumn of 2019, I decided to launch Nourish by Nisha, my very own café, to feed more people. It was a thrilling and enjoyable way to experience a real service kitchen, especially since it could fit perfectly into my weekday schedule while my children were at school, and left weekends for taking on private dining bookings.

The start of 2020 held so much promise and optimism for me, but the rug was abruptly pulled out from under my feet with the Covid pandemic. All the hard work I had put into building my business over the past two years came to a halt – no more private dining, no more café, no furlough, and no back-up plan. Everything ground to a standstill, leaving me without a financial safety net.

Like most people, I had to adjust to the monotony of staying home, working remotely, and homeschooling my children. But I stumbled upon something unexpected – I started recording and sharing my dinner creations with friends and family who were struggling with mealtime boredom. Encouraged by their positive responses, I began posting these tutorials online. It gave me a sense of routine and purpose as I got dressed in the morning, filmed my dishes, and edited them to make them Instagram-worthy. I was overwhelmed by the outpouring of gratitude from my followers, and it felt like my small contribution was making a difference during such a bizarre time. Through this, I built a thriving community of followers who regularly made my recipes. Before I knew it, I had grown a platform of 50,000 new followers.

My impact during that time was more than just being known for my culinary skills. People started reaching out to me with messages of gratitude like, 'You saved my marriage,' and 'My children finally like noodles.' I was moved by emotional messages too, such as, 'Your kheema reminded me of the way my mum used to make it, before she passed away.' It dawned on me that what I was providing was more than just food – it was comfort, joy, and cherished memories all rolled into one.

As we adapted to the 'new normal', my videos gradually faded away, and I began hosting more in-person events, like supper clubs. I even launched a pop-up Asian tearoom called The Secret Garden, which was inspired by the novel by Frances Hodgson Burnett. This serene garden was created to bring people together and promote healing after the tragedy of the pandemic.

With both cafés now closed, it's given me the opportunity to write this book. And while it's been wonderful to visit restaurants again, the period of unsociability has left me yearning for the simple pleasure of hosting people at home.

The ceremony of eating, drinking, laughing and talking makes me often say to friends: 'Come over, I'll cook – let's stay home.'

plan the perfect menu

The key components to consider when creating the menu are: numbers, time and season.

Cooking for two or twenty will definitely dictate the menu, with considerations about oven space, crockery, cutlery and the dreaded washing up! With larger numbers I tend to go for a hero centrepiece and lots of side dishes, or just one big pot of happiness and an easy dessert. You don't have to have a three-course dinner party – gone are the days when this is an expected norm. I like doing multiple courses for my clients, but rarely do I imitate this for dinner parties at home. I've offered some menu plan suggestions on pages 200-201.

I love the idea of presenting little snacks with a welcome drink while you spend the first half hour acclimatizing and catching up. A little morsel of deliciousness creates the anticipation of what's to come and gives you some time with your guests. The main aim is to spend maximum time with them, and not in the kitchen.

I also don't fall victim to the rule of same-cuisine symmetry. I am very happy to create something globally disjointed but one that delivers on flavour, texture and colour.

Everyone is short of time. So if you haven't been given much notice, my fallback plan is usually a couple of warm Camemberts, crusty bread, olives and charcuterie. Dessert can be shop-bought ice cream with some crushed ginger nuts and espresso, or some sliced oranges sprinkled with cinnamon, honey and pistachios.

We shouldn't make cooking for others such an anxious process. More times than not, they are coming to spend time with you, to soak up the atmosphere. Food is a bonus, but beautiful food does make people feel special. Once you've created your own rhythm of cooking for others, even just for the ones you live with, my hope is you will enjoy it.

Cooking seasonally usually helps me decide quickly what to centre my menu around. Eating this way helps keep the costs low, tastes better and there's an abundance of the ingredients available with a lower carbon footprint. Although I do not religiously follow this mantra, when I do the food often tastes effortlessly better.

Once you have considered the numbers, time and seasons, get yourself a notepad and jot everything down.

And if that doesn't work, ask yourself, 'What do I fancy eating?' Often I cook dinner out of pure greed, cravings and desire for what I want to eat, and this enthusiasm will ripple through the guests, who will all want to eat the same!

about this book

Imagine having a go-to cookbook for those special occasions when you want to cook something extraordinary – whether you're celebrating a big milestone, having a cozy Saturday night in, or catching up with loved ones. This is the book you'll reach for when you want to wow your mum, impress your friends, or simply enjoy a memorable meal. Say goodbye to stuffy three-course dinners with matching plates and linen napkins – the modern dinner party is all about relaxed, shared plates and snacky bits that bring people together for real-life conversations, laughter and clinking glasses. And with this cookbook, you'll have all the inspiration you need to create unforgettable moments and make lasting memories with the people you care about most. Don't forget to snap an obligatory selfie together to capture the moment!

small plates
& asian tapas

I rarely usher my guests straight to the dining table upon their arrival. Instead, there's a special moment of excitement and joy as we're reunited. I prefer to invite everyone into the kitchen, lounge or garden, where I offer a selection of drinks and we engage in lively conversation. We might enjoy a glass of Prosecco or a bottle of beer, or perhaps a special guava mocktail or rhubarb spritzer. Meanwhile, the snacks are already prepared and displayed beautifully on the kitchen counter or in the living room, waiting to delight my guests.

Even on days I haven't got guests coming round, on weekends I enjoy creating a sense of occasion. My children are also invested in this ritual. Fizzy pop with a cocktail umbrella for them and an Aperol spritz for me signals the start of the weekend – after all, what's more important than celebrating life for absolutely no reason at all?

Small snacks alongside a drink allow us time to unwind, setting the tone for more deliciousness ahead. Even if I haven't made anything from scratch, just having a few bowls of nuts, crisps and olives indicates pub vibes for me. Staying in really is the new going out!

The following ideas for snacks and Asian-inspired tapas have been on my private dining menus from the very beginning. My guests get really excited when these are served; it's the first promise of what's to come. Some of these dishes go well with drinks, while others can be used as a starter. Even making a selection of, say, four or five, would be enough to create a table of sharing tapas. I really want you to find your own style and be creative with these ideas to build a table of happiness!

red thai arancini

Leftovers are unsung heroes. I once had sticky jasmine rice and Thai curry
sauce left over, and stored in a container overnight they congealed together,
taking on the characteristics of leftover risotto. Over time I have tweaked
the recipe to achieve the perfect texture, and the heady taste of lemongrass
and lime leaf transport me to balmy evenings at a Bangkok night market.

Makes 25

2 tbsp rapeseed (canola) oil
1 large onion, diced
5 garlic cloves, crushed
2cm (¾-inch) piece of fresh ginger,
  peeled and grated
1 green finger chilli, finely chopped
2 lemongrass stalks, finely chopped
275g (10oz) Arborio rice
1 tbsp red Thai curry paste
400ml (14fl oz) hot vegetable or chicken
  stock (or 1 stock cube dissolved in
  400ml/14fl oz boiling water)
400ml (14fl oz) coconut milk
6 fresh makrut lime leaves, thinly sliced
6 spring onions (scallions), finely
  chopped
Small bunch of coriander (cilantro),
  finely chopped
Grated zest and juice of 1 lime
50g (1¾oz) Parmesan, grated
25g (1oz) butter
1 tsp caster (superfine) sugar
1 litre (34fl oz/4¼ cups) vegetable oil,
  for deep-frying
Salt, to taste
Sriracha mayo, to serve
Thai basil leaves (or coriander/cilantro
  if you don't have basil), to garnish

To assemble and cook
75g (2½oz) plain (all-purpose) flour
2 eggs, beaten
120g (4oz) panko breadcrumbs
1 tsp each of black and white
  sesame seeds

Heat the rapeseed oil in a pan, add the onion and sweat over
a medium heat for about 5 minutes, until translucent but not
browned. Add the garlic, ginger, chilli and lemongrass and cook
for a minute until fragrant. Add the rice and stir to ensure each
grain is coated in oil and aromatics. Now add the curry paste and
cook for a minute, ensuring each grain is coated.

In a separate pan, combine the hot stock and coconut milk; it
should be warm, so gently heat if not. A ladleful at a time, add
the liquid to the rice pan, stirring and letting each addition
absorb before adding the next, until all the liquid has been
absorbed and the rice is al dente. Add the lime leaves, spring
onions, coriander, lime zest and juice, Parmesan, butter and
sugar, and mix well. Season to taste with salt. Transfer to a wide
baking tray and refrigerate for at least 4 hours, or overnight.

Place the flour, beaten eggs and breadcrumbs in 3 separate
bowls. Add the sesame seeds to the breadcrumbs and mix well.
It's useful to use weighing scales to ensure uniform arancini,
although you can do it by eye. Divide the risotto into 25 equal
portions, each about the size of a golf ball or weighing 40g
(1½oz), and roll into balls. It helps to refrigerate for at least an
hour before breadcrumbing. Dip each ball in the flour, then the
egg, and finally the breadcrumbs. Transfer to a tray and set aside.

Heat the vegetable oil in a deep-fat fryer or in a large, heavy-
based saucepan (making sure it comes no more than halfway
up the sides) until it reads 170°C (338°F) on a cooking
thermometer, or a small piece of bread dropped into the oil turns
golden brown in 45 seconds. In batches, lower the risotto balls
into the oil and deep-fry for 6–8 minutes, or until golden brown.
Remove with a slotted spoon to a tray lined with kitchen paper.
If you are not serving straight away, they can be reheated in a
180°C/350°F/gas mark 4 oven for 10–12 minutes.

Serve the arancini with a touch of sriracha mayo and a Thai basil
leaf. Serve as a sharing platter, or 3 each as a starter.

nori tostadas with tajín

Something very exciting happens when you fry rice paper: it puffs up like a poppadom with the most extraordinary texture. The nori tostada is the one you pull out to impress… looks fancy but it's deceptively very simple. Another make-ahead dish that can be quickly assembled in front of your guests, this little crunchy morsel definitely has the wow factor.

Makes 16 mini tacos

4 sheets of nori seaweed
4 large round sheets of rice paper
500ml (17fl oz/generous 2 cups)
    vegetable oil, for deep-frying
150g (5¼oz) drained canned sweetcorn
2 spring onions (scallions), finely
    chopped
½ avocado, finely diced
2 tbsp mayonnaise
Squeeze of lime juice
1 tbsp tajín seasoning (or 1 tsp
    chilli flakes)

To garnish
Nigella seeds
Coriander (cilantro) cress (or finely
    chopped coriander)

Start by taking one nori sheet and one rice paper, brush a little water on the rice paper and stick the nori sheet to the rice paper. Using scissors, cut off any overhang and cut each into quarters.

Heat the vegetable oil in a deep-fat fryer or in a large, heavy-based saucepan (making sure it comes no more than halfway up the sides) until it reads 170°C (338°F) on a cooking thermometer, or a small piece of rice paper sizzles and expands immediately. Gently drop in 2 nori quarters at a time to the hot oil; they will puff and curl up almost instantly. Use a slotted spoon to flatten each, turn once, then remove immediately (they take no longer than 10 seconds to cook) and drain on kitchen paper.

While the nori crisps are cooling, mix together the sweetcorn, spring onions, avocado, mayonnaise, lime juice and tajín seasoning. Ensure any excess liquid is drained off, then pile into the nori tostada shells, garnish with nigella seeds and coriander cress and serve immediately.

bombay beetroot bubble

Chaat is my first memory of street food as a child. Chaat stalls are the social 'pubs' of buzzing cities like Mumbai and Delhi. The direct translation of chaat is 'to lick' – think finger-licking good! It's an addictive, complex balance of sweet, spicy, salty, crunchy and tangy.

Pani puri, or dhai puri, are little hollow semolina golf balls ready for a spicy water dunking (pani) or a gentle yogurt bathing. Traditionally these puris are filled with potatoes, but the accidental concoction here came about when I had a packet of beetroot in the fridge and no potatoes.

A medley of chutneys is the character of a good chaat. There is only one rule – eat the whole puri in one shot. Do not even attempt to bite it; the pleasure is in the whole puri exploding in your mouth like a flavour bomb! You can buy the shells in all Indian grocery stores and online. They are very fiddly to make at home and therefore Indians aways buy them too!

Makes 20–25

150g (5¼oz) Greek yogurt
2 tbsp honey or 1 tbsp caster
 (superfine) sugar
¼ tsp salt
2 cooked beetroots (beets), diced
 (or 1 boiled potato)
½ avocado, diced
¼ red onion, finely diced
60g (2oz) drained cooked chickpeas
 (from a can or jar)
1 tsp chaat masala
1 punnet of cooked pani puri
70g (2½oz) tamarind chutney (see page
 183 for homemade)
70g (2½oz) green chutney (see page
 184 for homemade coriander and
 mint chutney)

To garnish
30g (1oz) pomegranate seeds
Handful of sev (optional)
Coriander (cilantro) cress (or finely
 chopped coriander), optional

Mix together the yogurt and honey with the salt. Stir until dissolved, adding a splash of water to loosen if needed.

Toss together the beetroot, avocado, onion and chickpeas, adding the chaat masala and a pinch of salt.

Assemble the pani puri 5 minutes before you are ready to serve. They will not last long, and I find they are best eaten soon after assembling as the filling will make them soggy. They can be quickly filled when your guests arrive and are enjoying drinks.

Fill the pani puri with the beetroot and chickpea mixture first, followed by the yogurt, then some tamarind and green chutney. Garnish with pomegranate seeds and sev (if using) and finish with some coriander cress, if you like.

sea bass roti tacos

Tacos, kebabs or kathi rolls – every country has its own version of a wrap. Mine has been inspired by a roti wrap I had in Barbados. It may have Trinidadian origins; like 'doubles', this roti is filled with chickpeas and chutneys. Here I've taken Indian and Mexican vibes – a turmeric chapati with crispy fish and a kachumber, like a salsa. You can use a cookie cutter (8cm/3¼ inches) to make these into canapés, or make larger for a starter.

Makes 20 mini tacos

For the taco dough
2 tsp vegetable oil, plus extra for greasing
200g (7oz) chapati flour (or plain/
   all-purpose flour)
½ tsp ground turmeric
¼ tsp salt
½ tsp dried fenugreek leaves
   (kasoori methi)
75ml (5 tbsp) lukewarm water

For the pakora
4 fillets of skinless sea bass (about
   400g/14oz in total), sliced into
   mini strips
1 tbsp ginger and garlic paste
   (see page 180 for homemade)
¾ tsp salt
½ tsp ground turmeric
1 tsp Kashmiri chilli powder
½ tsp lemon juice
100g (3½oz) gram (chickpea) flour
¼ tsp ajwain (carom) seeds
About 75ml (5 tbsp) water
600ml (20fl oz/2½ cups) vegetable oil,
   for deep-frying

For the salsa
½ red onion, finely diced
½ cucumber, finely diced
½ red (bell) pepper, finely diced
¼ tsp lime juice
Small handful of coriander (cilantro),
   finely chopped
Salt, to taste

Avocado chutney (page 181), to serve
Lime wedges (optional), to serve

Make the dough by mixing the oil and chapati flour together in a bowl until sand-like. Add the turmeric, salt and fenugreek leaves, then gradually pour in the water, mixing with a fork. Bring the dough together with your hands, knead for 2–3 minutes until smooth, then form into a ball and spread a drop of oil over the surface to prevent it from cracking. Cover the bowl and leave to rest for at least 15 minutes.

Meanwhile, place the fish in a bowl with the ginger and garlic paste, ½ teaspoon salt, ¼ teaspoon of the turmeric, the chilli powder and lemon juice and mix to coat. Set aside to marinate.

Make the salsa by mixing all the ingredients together in a bowl.

Split the dough into 6 balls and roll them out into rounds as thinly as you can. You don't need a perfect circle because you will use a cookie cutter to cut out the mini tacos. Or, if you prefer, you can leave them as they are, for larger tacos. Using an 8cm (3¼-inch) plain cookie cutter, stamp out rounds of dough and cook them in batches in a dry frying pan for about 30 seconds on each side, flipping twice to ensure the underside is cooked and pressing gently with kitchen paper if needed. They will puff up on the second flip. Keep them warm wrapped in a tea towel.

For the pakora batter, mix the gram flour with the remaining ¼ teaspoon of turmeric and ¼ teaspoon of salt, and the ajwain seeds. Add the water until it reaches double (heavy) cream consistency. You can fry the pakora before the guests arrive and keep them warm in a low oven.

Heat the vegetable oil in a deep-fat fryer or in a large, heavy-based saucepan (making sure it comes no more than halfway up the sides) until it reads 180°C (356°F) on a cooking thermometer, or a small piece of bread dropped into the oil turns golden brown in 45 seconds.

Dip each strip of sea bass into the batter to coat, then lower into the oil
in batches and deep-fry for 2–3 minutes, until the batter starts to crisp up.
Remove and drain on kitchen paper.

To assemble the tacos, add some avocado chutney first, then the battered fish
and salsa. Serve on a taco stand, or leaning against each other. If you like, try
the lime wedges for extra wow factor!

japanese asparagus fritti

Italians call it fritti, the Japanese call it tempura. Anything that is deep-fried is glorious, one of God's gifts to make everything in the world better! It's almost like the forbidden fruit, ingrained in us that it's 'bad'! Well, in its defence, asparagus is a green vegetable, full of antioxidants – deep-fried, yes, but it still counts towards your five-a-day! So enjoy and devour guilt-free. This is the perfect snack for convo and cocktails.

Serves 4

2 bunches (500g/1lb 2oz) of asparagus
    spears, each cut on the diagonal into
    3 equal lengths (use fine green beans
    if asparagus is out of season)
600ml (20fl oz/2½ cups) rapeseed
    (canola) oil, for deep-frying
2 garlic cloves, finely sliced
Handful of shiso or Thai basil leaves
1 tsp shichimi togarashi, to garnish

For the batter
50g (1¾oz) plain (all-purpose) flour
60g (2oz) cornflour (cornstarch)
1 tsp baking powder
½ tsp salt
½ tsp ground white pepper
175ml (6fl oz) ice-cold sparkling water

For the yuzu mayo dip (optional)
4 tbsp mayonnaise
1 tsp yuzu juice (or lime juice)

For the batter, mix together the dry ingredients in a bowl, then add the ice-cold sparkling water and whisk until smooth and the consistency of double (heavy) cream. Drop the asparagus into the batter.

Heat the rapeseed oil in a deep-fat fryer or in a large, heavy-based saucepan (making sure it comes no more than halfway up the sides) until it reads 180°C (356°F) on a cooking thermometer, or a small piece of batter dropped into the oil sizzles nicely.

Add the garlic slices to the hot oil, which will cook in a matter of seconds. Stir gently and remove as soon as they are golden. Remove the asparagus from the batter and lower one at a time into the hot oil. Fry in small batches for a couple of minutes, turning gently until slightly golden and crispy. Remove with a slotted spoon to kitchen paper to drain. Dip the shisho leaves into the batter and fry in the hot oil for a minute, until crispy.

For the yuzu mayo dip (if using), mix the mayonnaise and yuzu together. Place the asparagus in a shallow sharing bowl, or individual bowls. Add the crispy leaves and garlic, shake over the shichimi togarashi and serve with the yuzu mayo dip.

{pictured right, overleaf}

crispy tofu pancakes

Tofu gets such a bad reputation but I truly believe it's only because people don't understand its personality. I adore tofu: it's a flavour sponge and very forgiving. This is the dish that will change your mind about tofu, I promise! Taking a popular Chinese institution of crispy duck and pancakes, you will make this vegan version of a takeaway classic on repeat for dinner parties and the family! It works equally well with shredded oyster mushrooms in place of tofu.

Makes 10

400g (14oz) firm tofu (bean curd)
    or 400g (14oz) oyster mushrooms,
    shredded
1½ tbsp Chinese five spice
1½ tbsp cornflour (cornstarch)
4 tbsp rapeseed (canola) oil
Sea salt and ground pepper, to taste

To serve
½ cucumber
5 spring onions (scallions)
1 packet (10–12) Chinese pancakes
    (shop-bought)
Hoisin sauce

First squeeze out any excess water from your tofu by wrapping in a clean tea (dish) towel or kitchen paper. Place something heavy on top and set aside for about 10 minutes.

In the meantime, cut your cucumber and spring onions into thin strips. I use a julienne peeler for the cucumber, discarding the watery middle (save to put in your next smoothie!).

Now cut your tofu into batons and coat in the five spice and cornflour, with salt and pepper to taste. Tofu is delicate, so be careful; I find using my fingers the best way. If using oyster mushrooms, follow the same process.

Heat the oil in a large frying pan and gently place each tofu baton in the hot oil, trying not to move it around too much. You are aiming for super-crispy edges, which will take about 7–8 minutes (same technique for the mushrooms). Once each side is crispy, remove and serve everything on a platter for your guests to assemble their own pancakes with some hoisin, spring onion, cucumber and tofu.

{pictured left, overleaf}

chilli paneer dumplings

If you have followed my page on Instagram for the last few years, chances are you bought this book for this recipe alone! These dumplings have a cult following: they are a huge favourite of Joe Wicks, and everyone has been asking me to share the recipe. I wanted to turn the elements of the Indo-Chinese dish chilli paneer into one of my favourite things of all to eat – a dim-sum-style dumpling. In the Himalayas they have momos, a Chinese-style dumpling with Indian undertones, using spices in the filling and served with a tomato-curry-style chutney.

You are welcome to make your own dumpling pastry (see page 178) but for the lazy cook in me, I love the convenient dumpling wrappers, often called gyoza skins, available in Asian supermarkets and online. The dumplings can be made in advance, then steamed just before guests arrive. If serving later, leave them in the steamer and gently reheat to serve.

Makes 30

4 tbsp vegetable oil
1 tbsp ginger and garlic paste (see page 180 for homemade)
5 spring onions (scallions), finely chopped
2 romano red peppers, deseeded and finely diced
100g (3½oz) mangetout, thinly sliced
1 tbsp light soy sauce
1 tsp dark soy sauce
1 tsp white pepper
½ tsp salt
230g (8oz) firm paneer, grated
30 gyoza wrappers (see page 178 for homemade)
Cornflour (cornstarch), for dusting

To serve
5 tbsp Chinkiang black vinegar
3 tbsp kecap manis
5 tbsp crispy chilli oil (see page 179 for homemade)
Small handful of coriander (cilantro) cress, to garnish

Heat the oil in a frying pan or wok, add the ginger and garlic paste and stir-fry over a medium-high heat for 20 seconds, then add the spring onions, peppers and mangetout and stir-fry for 4 minutes. Add the soy sauces, white pepper and salt, then remove from the heat and set aside to cool. Once cool, mix through the grated paneer and check for seasoning.

While the mixture is cooling, mix the black vinegar and kecap manis together in a bowl and set aside.

Spoon 1 heaped teaspoon of the filling onto the middle of each gyoza skin. Now begin to pleat the sides in a circular motion around the filling until all the edges come together into the middle. Pinch the top together to seal and place onto a plate dusted with cornflour and continue until you finish the filling and dumpling wrappers. Cover the dumplings with a damp tea towel to prevent them from drying out. If you need a visual guide to shaping the dumplings, I have a video on my Instagram showing how to do it.

You can now store the dumplings in the fridge for up to 8 hours, or steam them straight away. They can also be half-steamed at this point, then reheated in the steamer when guests arrive. In batches, arrange the dumplings in a steamer and steam for 10 minutes over a high heat.

Add 1 teaspoon of the soy-kecap-manis mixture to each bowl, arrange 3–5 dumplings on top and spoon over 1 teaspoon of crispy chilli oil. Garnish with a few strands of coriander cress and serve.

kimchi pakoras with gochujang yogurt

An Asian twist on the classic onion bhajia, everyone's favourite Indian restaurant starter, but with the addition of kimchi to ramp up the flavour and give an interesting texture. Perfect with a beer!

Makes about 20

250g (9oz) kimchi
150g (5¼oz) gram (chickpea) flour
1 tsp ground turmeric
1 tsp paprika
1 tsp ground coriander
1 tsp ground cumin
1 tsp fennel seeds
4 onions, finely sliced
Handful of kale or spinach,
  roughly chopped
½ tsp sea salt
250ml (1 cup) vegetable oil

For the dipping yogurt
½ tsp sugar
150g (5¼oz) Greek yogurt
1 tbsp gochujang paste

Drain the kimchi in a sieve set over a jug (pitcher) or bowl, and squeeze out as much liquid as possible. Measure the spicy liquid and top up with water to make it 150ml (5fl oz). Roughly chop the kimchi.

Add the gram flour and all the dried spices to a large bowl. Slowly whisk the diluted kimchi juice into the flour mixture to make a thick batter. Add the onions, kale, salt and kimchi and mix together.

Add the oil to a large, heavy-based saucepan and place over a medium heat until it reads 175°C (347°F) on a cooking thermometer, or a small amount of the pakora mixture dropped into the oil fizzes.

In batches, gently drop heaped tablespoons of pakora mixture into the hot oil and fry for 3–4 minutes, turning occasionally until golden brown. Remove to kitchen paper.

Mix the sugar into the yogurt and swirl through the gochujang, ready for pakora dipping.

Tip
For an extra crispy pakora, add 1 heaped tablespoon of rice flour.

lamb gyoza-samosa

Bit of a mouthful, but what a discovery! Gyoza wrappers double up as samosa wrappers, which is incredibly convenient if you're not skilled in the art of triangle origami! These crispy samosa hybrids feature a classic dry lamb mince filling, wrapped into a delightful half-moon shape that is sure to impress your guests. The only downside is that they are only two bites, so everyone may end up fighting over them!

Makes about 25

2 tsp plain (all-purpose) flour
2 tbsp water
25 gyoza wrappers (see page 178
   for homemade)
Vegetable oil, for deep-frying
Lime wedges or apple chutney
   (page 181), to serve

For the filling
15ml (1 tbsp) rapeseed (canola) oil
½ tsp cumin seeds
1 cinnamon stick
5 green cardamom pods
1 large onion, diced
2 green finger chillies, finely chopped
1 tsp garlic paste
1 tsp ginger paste
250g (9oz) lean minced (ground) lamb
1 tsp ground cumin
1 tsp ground coriander
½ tsp ground turmeric
1 tsp garam masala
½ tsp Kashmiri chilli powder
1 tsp sea salt
Juice of ½ lime
Handful of chopped coriander (cilantro)
50g (1¾oz) frozen peas, thawed

For the filling, warm the oil in a large pot over a low heat, then add the cumin seeds, cinnamon stick and cardamom pods. Let the seeds crackle for 30 seconds. Add the onion and sauté for about 5 minutes until translucent but not browned. Next, add the chillies and garlic and ginger pastes, and stir for a minute.

Turn up the heat slightly, add the minced lamb and sauté for about 5 minutes, breaking it up with a wooden spoon, then add all the ground spices and salt. Cook out for a few more minutes until evenly browned.

Turn down the heat, squeeze in the lime juice, cover and cook for another 10 minutes. The mixture should be quite dry. Finally, add the chopped coriander and the peas, stir and leave to cool. Check for seasoning and remove the cinnamon stick and cardamom pods. Mix the flour with the water to make a 'glue', thick enough to coat the back of a spoon but still spreadable.

Grab a gyoza wrapper and spoon some filling over one half. Spread some 'glue' on the other half semi-circle and fold the wrapper over, pressing down to create a half-moon shape. Repeat with the remaining wrappers and filling. You can now store these in the fridge, or fry immediately. You can fry them in advance and then reheat them in the oven when your guests arrive, but they will lose a bit of crispness.

Heat enough vegetable oil to come halfway up the sides of a large, heavy-based saucepan or deep-fat fryer, and place over a medium heat until it reads 160°C (320°F) on a cooking thermometer, or when a small piece of bread dropped into the oil sizzles within 5 seconds. In batches, deep-fry the samosas for 2–3 minutes, turning occasionally, until golden brown. Remove and drain well on kitchen paper before serving, with lime wedges or apple chutney.

edamame & truffle gyoza

The inspiration for these dumplings – one of my first recipes for my private dining menus – was a bag of edamame beans in the freezer and a vegan guest who couldn't eat my paneer dumplings. I blitzed the beans with some aromatics but still felt like it needed depth of flavour. Mushrooms always add umami but risked making the mixture too watery. Truffle paste came to the rescue and worked wonderfully against the sweetness of the edamame.

Makes 12–14

200g (7oz) frozen edamame beans
1 garlic clove, crushed
2cm (¾-inch) piece of fresh ginger, peeled and grated
1 heaped tbsp truffle paste (or miso)
1 tbsp truffle oil
2 tbsp light soy sauce
12–14 gyoza wrappers (see page 178 for homemade)
2 tsp vegetable oil
3 spring onions (scallions), finely chopped, to garnish

For the dipping sauce
5 tbsp light soy sauce
2 tbsp toasted sesame oil
2 tbsp rice wine vinegar
½ tsp white sesame seeds
½ tsp chilli flakes or chilli oil (optional; see page 179 for homemade)

First make the dipping sauce by mixing all the ingredients together, then set aside until ready to serve.

Cook the edamame in boiling water for 5 minutes, then drain. Add to a food processor with the garlic, ginger, truffle paste, truffle oil and soy sauce, and pulse until combined but coarse.

Have a small bowl of water ready, and grab a gyoza wrapper. Using your finger, run water around the edge of the wrapper. Spoon 1 heaped teaspoon of the filling onto the middle the wrapper. Fold the wrapper in half over the filling and pinch it in the centre with your thumb and index finger (but don't seal yet!). Using your right thumb and index finger, start making a pleat about once every 5mm (¼ inch) on the top part of the wrapper from the centre towards the right. Once you have made 3–4 pleats, continue with the left side of the gyoza, pleating from the centre towards the left. Pinch the top to seal. Repeat with the remaining wrappers and filling. (You can refer to my dumpling masterclass video on YouTube for visual guidance.) These can now be stored in the fridge on a cornflour-dusted surface, covered with a damp tea (dish) towel to prevent them drying out.

When ready to cook, place a 30cm (12-inch) non-stick frying pan that has a lid over a medium heat and add 2 teaspoons of oil. Add the dumplings to the pan and brown on both sides. Now add 150ml (5fl oz) water, cover and wait until the water has completely evaporated and the dumplings are soft and plump.

Take off the heat and place on a dinner plate. Garnish with the spring onions and serve with the dipping sauce.

spicy teriyaki blistered padrón & edamame

This is one bowl of greens that brings everyone joy – even children! There is something so playful about bursting the edamame beans from the pod or holding a miniature Padrón pepper by its stalk. Ideally, this is made with Japanese shishito peppers but they aren't as widely available as Padrón peppers. These snacks delight and give you that restaurant feeling at home. Leave out the sriracha for a mild version – my kids devour these!

Serves 4

250g (9oz) edamame beans in
   pods (frozen)
250g (9oz) Padrón peppers
Toasted sesame seeds, to garnish
   (optional)

For the spicy teriyaki sauce
2 tbsp light soy sauce
1 garlic clove, crushed
1 tbsp sesame oil
1 tbsp sriracha
1 tbsp honey
1 tsp brown sugar

In a screw-top jar or bowl, mix together all the ingredients for the spicy teriyaki sauce. If using a jar, close with the lid and shake vigorously. Set aside.

Steam the frozen edamame beans for about 7 minutes.

Add the Padrón peppers to a dry frying pan over a medium heat. Let them blister evenly without moving the pan too much. Add the steamed edamame to the pan to blister slightly (this will give them a smoky flavour and exciting appearance). The peppers are done once they are blistered and slightly wrinkled.

Now add the sauce and let it bubble for a minute or so, then serve immediately, sprinkling over some toasted sesame seeds, if desired. If making in advance, add the sauce at the last minute to heat through.

sweet potato & cumin wontons

Sweet potatoes are a beloved staple in our household. I often grate them
into breakfast fritters, and once I overestimated and grated too much…
from which came the idea of stuffing them into a dumpling. The contrast
of sweet potato against the chilli oil makes these moreish little morsels so
addictive. A very easy dumpling that can be made in under an hour for an
impressive restaurant-style dish. Serve individually in bowls or on a big
platter for everyone to share.

Makes 20–25

1 tbsp rapeseed (canola) oil
2.5cm (1-inch) piece of fresh ginger,
  peeled and grated
2 garlic cloves, crushed
1 red chilli, finely diced
2 large sweet potatoes, peeled and
  grated (about 400g/14oz in total)
3 spring onions (scallions), finely
  chopped
1 tbsp dark soy sauce
1 tbsp vegan oyster sauce
½ tsp ground cumin
Pinch of ground white pepper
Pinch of salt
20–25 frozen wonton wrappers, thawed
Handful of coriander (cilantro) stalks,
  finely chopped

For the dressing
2 tbsp light soy sauce
2 tbsp Chinkiang black vinegar
1 tsp sesame oil
1 tsp chilli oil (see page 179
  for homemade)

Heat the rapeseed oil in a wide frying pan or wok over a medium
heat, add the ginger, garlic and chilli and stir-fry for about
2 minutes until the aromatics are released. Now add the grated
sweet potato and spring onions, cook for about a minute, then
add the soy sauce, oyster sauce, cumin, white pepper and salt.
Cook for 2 minutes until the liquid is absorbed. Remove from
the heat and leave to cool slightly.

Meanwhile, make the dressing by combining all the ingredients
in a bowl. Set aside.

Have a small bowl of water ready to seal the wontons. Place a
wonton wrapper on a flat surface, covering the rest with a damp
tea (dish) towel to prevent them drying out. Place 1 heaped
teaspoon of filling mixture in the middle of the wrapper. Wet
your finger and run it around the edge of the wrapper, now twist
the edges up together to meet at the top and pinch. Repeat with
the remaining filling and wrappers.

To cook the wontons, bring a wide pot of water to the boil,
drop in the wontons, in batches if necessary, and simmer for
5 minutes. Using a large slotted spoon or sieve, remove and
transfer straight into the chilli oil dressing to coat. Once all the
wontons have been coated, serve in a large bowl or platter, or in
individual bowls. Sprinkle over the coriander stalks and serve
with chopsticks.

{pictured right, overleaf}

malaysian jackfruit coconut curry puffs with apple chutney

Believed to be inspired by the Cornish pasty, the curry puff was introduced to the Malay Peninsula in the 1800s, although some have suggested that the shape of the curry puff is similar to a Portuguese empanada. My original curry puff was filled with my samosa lamb mince recipe as seen on MasterChef, but I adapted it to a vegan version when I hosted a charity event to help families who look after jackfruit crops in India. Jackfruit has a meaty texture and the ability to suck up flavours like a sponge! The sweet tropical notes of coconut and earthy curry powder here are toned down by the fresh apple chutney. A complex yet familiar combination which some might say tastes like a pimped-up sausage roll!

Makes 8

3 tbsp coconut (or rapeseed) oil
1 tsp cumin seeds
8 fresh curry leaves
1 medium onion, diced
1 tbsp ginger and garlic paste (see page 180 for homemade)
2 green finger chillies, finely chopped
1 x 400g (14oz) can of young green jackfruit (do not get ripe jackfruit!), drained and roughly chopped
1 tbsp medium curry powder
1 tbsp light soy sauce
3 tbsp coconut milk
1 heaped tbsp fine desiccated (fine dried shredded) coconut
30g (1oz) frozen peas, thawed
Small bunch of coriander (cilantro), chopped
1 x 300g (10½oz) ready-rolled sheet of puff pastry
Salt and sugar, to taste
Apple chutney (see page 181), to serve

To glaze and coat
5 tbsp coconut milk
Generous pinch of ground turmeric
20g (¾oz) black sesame seeds

In a pan over a low–medium heat, melt the coconut oil then add the cumin seeds. Let them sizzle for a few seconds, then add the curry leaves until they splutter. Add the onion and sauté for 5–6 minutes until light brown, then add the ginger and garlic paste and green chillies. Cook out for 30 seconds.

Add the chopped jackfruit, followed by the curry powder, soy sauce and coconut milk. Cover and cook over a low heat for about 10 minutes, so that the spices lose their 'rawness'.

Add the desiccated coconut and peas, with salt and sugar to taste. Cook for 2 minutes until the coconut is coated in the spices, then finish with the coriander and set aside to cool.

Preheat the oven to 200°C/400°F/gas mark 6.

Divide the pastry evenly into 8 squares. Add about 1 tablespoon of the cooled filling mixture to the middle of each square. Fold a bottom corner towards its opposite corner to meet at the top, then pinch along all the seams to close up the puffs, eliminating any trapped air as you go. Place on a baking tray and brush with the coconut milk mixed with the turmeric. Sprinkle the sesame seeds on top and pop into the oven for 25 minutes, until risen and evenly golden brown. Serve with the chutney.

{pictured left, overleaf}

bombay crab crumpets with avocado chutney & poppadom crumbs

Inspired by a restaurant in Mumbai called Trishna, which specializes in garlic butter crab, I've taken the ultimate indulgence of sweet crab meat and added a British base of a crisp, airy crumpet. An elegant snack, or even a starter, without the messy struggle of the crab shells! The crushed poppadoms give a divine crunch to the dish. For canape-sized crumpets, I use a cookie cutter to make smaller versions – you should be able to get 2 canapes from each crumpet. Using a full-sized crumpet makes the perfect starter, if preferred.

Serves 6

150g (5¼oz) unsalted butter
1 tsp fennel seeds
4 tsp crushed garlic
2 tsp finely chopped green finger chillies
4 tsp freshly ground black pepper
300g (10½oz) picked white crab meat
40g (1½oz) picked brown crab meat
2 tbsp lime juice, plus extra to serve
Handful of coriander (cilantro) leaves,
    plus extra to serve
6 crumpets (shop-bought)
3 poppadoms
Sea salt
Avocado chutney (page 181), to serve

In a wide, non-stick pan over a medium heat, heat the butter for 2 minutes, with a splash of water added to ensure the butter doesn't burn, until a frothy emulsion is created. Add the fennel seeds to sizzle for a few seconds, then add the garlic, chillies and black pepper, and cook out for a few minutes. Add both crab meats, stir, then lower the heat, cover and simmer for 5 minutes. Once the crab has absorbed most of the liquid, remove from the heat, season with salt and add the lime juice and coriander leaves.

Meanwhile, toast your crumpets (or for extra crispness and flavour, spread butter on each side and pan-fry until golden brown).

Roast the poppadoms over a high heat then, once cool, crush them with your hands into crumbs.

To serve, spread avocado chutney on each crumpet and pile the crab on top. Garnish with poppadom crumbs and coriander, with a squeeze of lime.

Tip
Leftover crumpet overhangs can be used as croutons to scatter over salads. Simply stir-fry in olive oil over a high heat until crispy and season. Alternatively use my za'atar pitta croutons method on page 119.

crispy potato maru bhajia

These crispy potato slices, known as Maru bhajia, originated in the renowned restaurant Maru in Nairobi, Kenya. They hold a special place in the hearts of East African Indians, including my father, who immigrated to Wembley, London, in the 1970s (interestingly, some members of the Maru family also settled in Wembley during the same era). As a child, I fondly remember accompanying my parents to Ealing Road in Wembley, the go-to place for Indian groceries. My parents would entice me to join them by treating me to a plate of piping-hot crispy bhajia at the Maru Bhajia House, accompanied by chutney and fresh passionfruit juice. Those experiences were truly unforgettable, and to this day these bhajia bring me immense joy and transport me back to that small restaurant with its humble seven tables.

Have the potato slices ready, soaking in cold water and keep the dry flour mixture prepped, then fry just before your guests arrive.

Serves 4

4 medium potatoes, such as Maris Piper
6 tbsp gram (chickpea) flour
2 tbsp rice flour
2 tsp cornflour (cornstarch)
2 tbsp grated fresh ginger
2 tbsp chopped green finger chillies
2 tsp ground turmeric
2 tsp ajwain (carom) seeds
2 tbsp finely chopped coriander
  (cilantro)
1 tsp salt
Pinch of sugar
2 tbsp lemon juice
Vegetable oil, for deep-frying
Tomato chutney (see page 178), to serve

Peel and thinly slice the potatoes, ideally using a mandoline, then immediately add them to a bowl of ice-cold water, to remove excess starch and make them extra crispy.

Meanwhile, in another bowl, mix the flours with the remaining ingredients, except the lemon juice and oil.

Drain the potatoes but do not pat dry; the excess water will help the flour mixture stick to them.

Add the flour coating to the potatoes, then the lemon juice, and combine, using your hands. Leave to stand for 10 minutes.

Half-fill a large, heavy-based saucepan with vegetable oil and place over a medium heat until it reads 190°C (374°F) on a cooking thermometer, or a little drop of batter added to the oil sizzles.

In batches, carefully add potato slices one at a time and deep-fry for about 2 minutes on each side, until golden. Remove and drain on kitchen paper, then serve with the tomato chutney.

sesame halloumi with chilli honey

Always have a block of halloumi in your fridge. It keeps for up to a year and is so versatile, including to whip up quick bites like this when you have friends popping over. Ready in 7 minutes, have this in your armoury to impress!

Serves 4

1 block (250g/9oz) of halloumi, cut into
   2cm (¾-inch) cubes
1 red chilli, finely chopped
2 tbsp runny honey (or maple syrup)
1 tsp mixture of toasted white and black
   sesame seeds
Finely chopped mint leaves (optional)

Heat a frying pan over a high heat, add the halloumi cubes and cook, stirring occasionally for about 2–3 minutes, until browned (you don't need to brown each side of every cube). Add the chilli and honey (or maple syrup), take off the heat and sprinkle over the sesame seeds.

Transfer to a small plate or bowl, scatter over the mint and serve with cocktail sticks.

beautiful
plates

If you had told me that one day I'd be whipping up
meals in the kitchens of footballers, pop stars and TV
personalities, I would have laughed it off. I mean, jobs
like that were surely reserved for Michelin-starred
chefs, right? It seemed like a far-fetched dream, but
life has a funny way of surprising us. And here I am,
inviting you to indulge in my Instagram grid, where
I reveal some of my top-secret signature dishes that
have won the hearts of famous clients. Some of these
dishes are not your everyday meals; they require extra
effort, but the end result is worth it.

I've also included some effortless showstoppers that
are less time consuming and which I often serve at
home on the weekends for family, or at dinner parties
for friends.

Treat yourself to a therapeutic cooking experience
with dishes that have received the coveted 'famous'
seal of approval! Join me in experiencing the joy
and magic of cooking something extra-special,
and let my signature dishes be a part of your own
feasting memories.

aubergine tarte tatin

I served this dish of marinated harissa aubergines in puff pastry in the magnificent St Paul's Cathedral, London, as part of a Christmas charity gala. It looks so impressive, yet it's a super-simple baked delight. Drizzle over the beautiful green tahini to bring the tart to life! Serve with roast potatoes and seasonal greens, or salad leaves in summer.

Serves 4

1 large or 2 small aubergines (eggplants)
3 tbsp rose harissa
2 tbsp olive oil
1 sheet of ready-rolled puff pastry
Sea salt
1 tbsp runny honey, to serve

For the green tahini sauce
60g (2oz) runny tahini
1 garlic clove, crushed
30g (1oz) coriander (cilantro) or
   parsley leaves
2 tbsp lemon juice

To garnish
Mint leaves, finely chopped
A few pomegranate seeds (optional)

Cut the aubergines into 2cm (¾-inch) discs (you need about 8 discs in total), rub a little salt over each, then rub the harissa paste all over them, adding 1 tablespoon of the olive oil to help spread it.

Add the remaining oil to a large ovenproof frying pan, about 26cm (10 inches) in diameter and place over a medium heat. Add the aubergine slices in a single layer and cook, turning for about 10 minutes, until slightly browned on both sides and softened slightly. Remove from the heat.

Preheat the oven to 200°C/400°F/gas mark 6.

Lay out the pastry on a flat surface and cut a circle a little larger than the pan, allowing for shrinkage. Carefully drape the pastry over the aubergines, tucking in the edges around the edge. Prick a few holes using a sharp knife, to allow the steam out, and transfer to the oven. Bake for 25–30 minutes, until the pastry has risen and is golden. (You can prepare the tart up to the point it goes in the oven and refrigerate until ready to cook, increasing the baking time by 10 minutes.)

Meanwhile, blitz the ingredients for the green tahini sauce together in a small food processor, adding a splash of water for pouring consistency.

Remove the tart from the oven and leave to stand for 5 minutes. Grab a plate big enough to cover the pan and, taking care to protect your hands from the heat, flip the tart upside down onto the plate.

Drizzle the tart with the honey and green tahini sauce and garnish with mint and pomegranate seeds, if desired.

keralan monkfish & clams with samphire pakoras

When I'm dreaming of the beach, I make this. A love letter from the tropics, as simple as ever, yet the delicate notes let the fish take centre stage. Clams infuse the broth with a beautiful depth, but even without the clams the coconut and curry leaves sing in harmony. This is delicious alone or paired with the cumin rice on page 185.

Serves 4

Vegetable oil, for frying
4 monkfish tails or any firm white fish fillets (hake, halibut, cod, tilapia or sea bass), each about 100g (3½oz)

For the Keralan coconut moilee sauce
1 tbsp coconut oil
2 tbsp yellow mustard seeds
20 fresh curry leaves
1 large onion, finely chopped
1 tsp ground turmeric
2 green finger chillies, finely chopped
2 tbsp peeled, grated fresh ginger
4 garlic cloves, crushed
800ml (27fl oz) coconut milk
200g (7oz) or 3 handfuls of scrubbed and washed clams (or mussels)
Generous squeeze of lime juice
Handful of coriander (cilantro), chopped, plus extra (optional) to garnish
Sugar and sea salt, to taste

For the samphire pakoras (optional)
3 tbsp gram (chickpea) flour
1 tbsp rice flour
¼ tsp ground turmeric
¼ tsp chilli powder
¼ tsp ajwain (carom) seeds
25ml (1½ tbsp) water
75g (2½oz) samphire

Heat the coconut oil in a large saucepan, add the mustard seeds and cook until they start to splutter. Add the curry leaves, let them sizzle, then turn down the heat before adding the onion. Cook for about 10 minutes until soft and translucent. Add the turmeric, chillies, ginger and garlic and stir to coat the onion in the spices. Pour in the coconut milk, add the clams and bring to the boil, then reduce to a simmer, cover and cook for 5 minutes until all the clams have opened. Add the lime juice and coriander, then season to taste with sugar and salt. Cover and leave to stand, ready to heat up when you serve.

If making the samphire pakoras (an Indian version of tempura), mix all the ingredients except the samphire in a bowl, adding salt to taste. The batter should be the consistency of double (heavy) cream. Heat enough vegetable oil to come halfway up the sides of a large, heavy-based saucepan or deep-fat fryer, and place over a medium heat until it reads 180°C (356°F) on a cooking thermometer, or a drop of batter added to the oil sizzles immediately. Dip the samphire sprigs into the batter and deep-fry in batches for a couple of minutes. Remove to kitchen paper to drain, and serve immediately or keep warm in a low oven.

Coat the fish fillets in oil, season lightly and place skin-side down in a non-stick frying pan over a medium heat. Cook for 3–4 minutes until you see the flesh turning opaque, then flip and cook the other side for 2–3 minutes, adding a knob of butter to caramelize and baste the fish. Remove from the pan and let rest for 5 minutes before serving.

To plate up, place some warmed sauce in the base of each bowl with a few clam shells for decoration (remove some shells as the clams will have fallen out). Carefully place the fish in the middle and garnish with the crispy samphire pakora, if serving. Garnish with coriander, if desired.

whole cauliflower shawarma with pistachio yogurt

Make this impressive cauliflower for a midweek dinner or as a fuss-free centrepiece to wow your guests. You can buy a shop-bought shawarma mix for ease, or make your own from the spices below. Serve on top of couscous or wrap it all up in a flatbread. It also makes a lovely side dish for roast chicken or with a couple of the layered salads for a mezze experience.

Serves 2–3

1 large cauliflower
1 packet of mixed grains or couscous (soaked in vegetable stock) or shop-bought pittas or flatbreads, to serve
Pomegranate seeds (optional but pretty!), to garnish

For the shawarma paste
50ml (2fl oz) melted butter
50ml (2fl oz) olive oil
3 garlic cloves, crushed
1 tsp sweet smoked paprika
1 tsp cayenne pepper (or Kashmiri chilli powder)
1 tsp ground coriander
1 tsp ground cumin
1 tsp ground turmeric
1 tsp ground allspice
½ tsp ground cinnamon
Juice of ½ lemon

For the pistachio yogurt
75g (2½oz) coriander (cilantro) stalks and leaves
40g (1½oz) shelled pistachios
2 garlic cloves, peeled
2 tbsp lemon juice
250g (9oz) Greek yogurt
Sea salt, to taste

For the salad
¼ red cabbage, shredded
2 little gem lettuces, sliced
2 carrots, grated
1 red onion, finely sliced
Handful of mild Lombardi pickled peppers (from a jar)
Handful of mint leaves
½ lemon, for squeezing
Tahini, to drizzle

Preheat the oven to 200°C/400°F/gas mark 6.

Remove the outer leaves from the cauliflower, keeping some back. Bring a large pan of water to the boil, add the cauliflower and blanch for 5 minutes, then drain and leave for 5 minutes to dry out and cool a little.

Mix all the ingredients for the shawarma paste together and rub it all over the cauliflower. Place in a baking tray, with the reserved leaves, and roast for 40 minutes.

Meanwhile, make the pistachio yogurt. Blitz the coriander (saving a few leaves to garnish), pistachios (save a few, chopped, to garnish), garlic, lemon juice and yogurt together. Season with salt to taste and set aside.

Mix together the salad vegetables and mint in a bowl, squeeze over the lemon and drizzle over some tahini.

Heat the grains (if using), or soak the couscous in vegetable stock, or warm the pittas or flatbreads.

Serve the cauliflower on a platter, topped with a drizzle of the pistachio yogurt, the reserved coriander leaves and chopped pistachios, and pomegranate seeds (if using).

Tip
Prepare all the elements before roasting the cauliflower for half the given time, finishing the cooking once your guests arrive.

ebi katsu curry

The moment I had my first taste of katsu curry, I couldn't help but wonder if it had Indian origins. It is believed that the British introduced the dish to Japan, bringing with them the culinary influence from India. The British navy had adopted this dish for their sailors during long sea voyages. In Japan, they adapted the curry by making it thicker and incorporating ingredients such as potatoes and meat. Prawns (shrimp) feel quite luxurious for a dinner party, so here is my ebi katsu, made with large prawns posing in their magnificent glory with the glossy curry sauce as their backdrop.

Serves 4

16 king tail-on prawns (jumbo shrimp), deveined
300g (10½oz) basmati rice, soaked in cold water
50g (1¾oz) plain (all-purpose) flour, seasoned
2 eggs, beaten
150g (5¼oz) panko breadcrumbs
Vegetable oil, for deep-frying
Sea salt

For the curry sauce
3 tbsp rapeseed (canola) oil
2 medium onions, diced
2 carrots, diced
2.5cm (1-inch) piece of fresh ginger, peeled and grated
4 garlic cloves, crushed
Handful of coriander (cilantro) stalks
2 heaped tsp medium curry powder
1 level tsp garam masala
1 heaped tsp plain (all-purpose) flour
300ml (10fl oz/1¼ cups) water or vegetable stock
1 tbsp light soy sauce
1 tbsp mango chutney

Quick pickled onion and chilli, to garnish (optional)
2 red chillies, sliced
1 red onion, sliced
Juice of 1 lime
Pinch of salt
½ tsp sugar

To serve
Salad leaves, tomatoes, cucumber
Thai sweet chilli sauce or olive oil
Sesame seeds, for sprinkling

If serving the pickled onion and chilli garnish, mix the ingredients together in a bowl and set aside.

Use a sharp knife and score a criss-cross pattern along the underside of each prawn, stopping before the tail tip and making sure you don't cut right through. Straighten each prawn by pressing it gently against the work surface.

Make the katsu sauce. Heat the oil in a pan over a medium heat, add the onions and carrots and sauté for 2–3 minutes until soft and translucent. Add the ginger, garlic and coriander stalks and cook out for a minute. Tip in the ground spices and the flour. The mixture will turn slightly thick at this stage. Stir in the water or stock and let simmer for about 10 minutes. Blitz using a stick blender, adding more water if necessary to achieve the right consistency. Finally, add the soy sauce and mango chutney, and salt if needed. Put back on the heat and leave on a gentle simmer.

While the sauce is cooking, drain the rice and add to a pan with 600ml (20fl oz) water. Bring to the boil over a high heat, then turn down to low and cook, covered, for 10 minutes, until all the water is absorbed. Remove from the heat and set aside.

Meanwhile, heat enough vegetable oil to come halfway up the sides of a large, heavy-based saucepan or deep-fat fryer, and place over a medium heat until it reads 180°C (356°F) on a cooking thermometer, or a few breadcrumbs dropped into the oil turn golden brown and sizzle immediately. While the oil is heating, create the breadcrumbing station. Put the flour, beaten eggs and breadcrumbs into 3 shallow bowls. Dip the prawns into the flour, then egg, then breadcrumbs and deep-fry, in batches, for 2–3 minutes until golden brown, moving them around gently for an even colour. Remove and keep warm.

Prepare a simple salad of mixed leaves or whatever you prefer. You can dress this in Thai sweet chilli sauce or just some olive oil.

Serve the rice by filling a bowl and turning it upside down in a mound on each serving plate. Sprinkle with sesame seeds, then arrange the prawns and salad, and pour some katsu sauce on the side, or let everyone help themselves. Scatter over the pickled onion and chilli, if using.

dan dan noodles with cucumber

Sitting on a tiny plastic stool, in the chaos of a Hong Kong night market, I was slurping these noodles and I couldn't figure out why my lips and tongue were tingling, but in a good way. This is the first time I came across Sichuan peppercorns; they are tangy with a pleasant lip-numbing effect that makes their flavour addictive.

Legend has it that there was a hawker who would carry a pole ('dan') on his shoulders up and down the streets in the province of Sichuan where this dish originates. Attached to each end were baskets, one containing handmade noodles and the other containing the sauce. Make this dish for your guests and I promise they will be addicted too.

Serves 4

4 nests of noodles of your choice, each 100g (3½oz) – I like ramen noodles or flower petal noodles

For the spicy dan dan sauce
7 garlic cloves, crushed
3 tbsp Korean gochugaru chilli flakes (or regular chilli flakes)
2 tbsp toasted, ground Sichuan peppercorns
8 tbsp vegetable oil
8 tbsp light soy sauce
2 tbsp Chinkiang black vinegar
4 tbsp tahini (or peanut butter)
4 tbsp soft brown sugar

For the mince
1 tbsp vegetable oil
200g (7oz) minced (ground) meat or meat alternative of your choice (chicken, pork, soya or crumbled tofu)
4 spring onions (scallions), chopped
1 tbsp ginger and garlic paste (see page 180 for homemade)
1 tsp Chinese five spice
1 tbsp light soy sauce
1 tbsp Shaoxing wine or rice wine (optional)
Pinch of freshly ground black pepper

To garnish
Cucumber, cut into julienne strips
Black and white sesame seeds

Start by making the dan dan sauce. In a heatproof bowl, combine the garlic, chilli flakes and Sichuan peppercorns. Heat the oil in a pan until little bubbles start to rise up, then carefully pour it over the aromatics. Stir in the soy sauce, black vinegar, tahini (or peanut butter) and sugar. Set aside.

For the mince, heat the oil in a frying pan or wok over a high heat, add the mince and stir-fry for 7–8 minutes, until just crisp. Add the spring onions with the ginger and garlic paste and stir-fry for 1 minute, then add the five spice, soy and rice wine. Stir for 5 minutes, then season with the black pepper and set aside.

Boil your noodles of choice, drain (saving the cooking water) and place portions in wide bowls. Add a few tablespoons of the saved cooking water to the dan dan sauce to thin it out, and warm it through slightly.

At this point you can start to assemble, or keep all the components separate until your guests arrive.

Add about 2 tablespoons of dan dan sauce to each bowl of noodles (less if you prefer it milder, more for spicier). Top with the mince, cucumber and a garnish of sesame seeds. Let everyone mix the noodles at the table.

If you are assembling later, simply dunk your cooked noodles in boiling water for a minute and heat the mince through; crisper mince actually works well in this recipe!

{pictured right, overleaf}

korean chicken bao buns – a cheat's version

I am obsessed with bao buns, the ultimate Asian burger. A pillowy half-moon submarine ready to be filled with hot and cold fillings with sauces, it's a handheld flavour bomb. Originating in China, the bao bun has gained red-carpet status and is now famous around the world.

By all means make your own bao buns (see page 177), but when I get a bao bun craving I want them immediately and refuse to wait 24 hours to let them prove! These are great snacks or you can make it into a full meal with my Vietnamese street fries (see page 96) for your next dinner party. They really do inject fun into any gathering and, using my shortcuts, this street-food phenomenon has never been easier. See below for a veggie alternative to chicken.

Serves 6

12 good-quality breadcrumbed chicken goujons
12 frozen bao buns (or see page 177 for homemade)
Kewpie mayonnaise (or normal mayonnaise)
½ cucumber, julienned, cut into wafer-thin slices
1 tbsp sesame seeds
2 spring onions (scallions), thinly sliced

For the Korean sauce
3 tbsp gochujang paste
2 tbsp dark soy sauce
2 tbsp honey
1 tbsp sesame oil

First combine all the sauce ingredients in a bowl and set aside. Prepare the cucumber and spring onions for garnish.

Next, cook the chicken goujons according to the packet instructions.

Steam the bao buns for 4–5 minutes. Meanwhile, slice the chicken goujons and mix them through the Korean sauce.

Now you are ready to assemble or let your guests create their own. I squeeze over a drizzle of mayonnaise first, followed by the cucumber, chicken, a scattering of sesame seeds and then the spring onions.

Veggie alternative with cauliflower
Divide a small cauliflower into florets. Mix together 100g (3 ½ oz) plain (all-purpose) flour, 2 tbsp cornflour (cornstarch) and about 150ml (5fl oz) ice-cold sparkling water and a pinch of salt; it should be the consistency of single (light) cream. Dip the florets in the batter to coat and deep-fry in oil heated to 180°C (356°F) for 3 minutes until golden. Remove and rest for 2 minutes before coating in the sauce and cramming into the buns (or serve with rice).

{pictured left, overleaf}

hariyali chicken biriyani traybake

A whole roast chicken always indicates celebration: it's a bold statement and everyone thinks you've gone to so much effort. This is a brilliant prep-ahead dish, with luxurious flavours and minimal washing up. Most are familiar with the bright-red tandoori or orange-tinged tikka marinades. Here I give the fiery hues a tranquil green makeover. This has all the Indian flavours of your familiar favourite, with herby harmonies that are so delicious you might never go back to sunset tikka again!

Serves 4

1 large chicken (or 8 bone-in thighs)
Sea salt, to taste

For the marinade
50g (1¾oz) coriander (cilantro) leaves
    and stalks
50g (1¾oz) mint leaves
30g (1oz) tarragon leaves (optional)
30g (1oz) basil leaves
8 garlic cloves, peeled
1 thumb-sized piece of fresh ginger,
    peeled and roughly chopped
3 green finger chillies
75g (2½oz) Greek yogurt
1 tbsp ground cumin
1 tbsp ground coriander
1 tsp garam masala
Juice of 1 lemon
2 medium onions, thinly sliced

For the rice
300g (10½oz) basmati rice
7 green cardamom pods
1 cinnamon stick
Few strands of saffron
¼ tsp ground turmeric
150ml (5fl oz) water

To garnish
Chopped coriander (cilantro
Pomegranate seeds (optional)

To serve
Poppadoms
Greek yogurt swirled with lime pickle

Spatchcock your chicken by removing the backbone (I use kitchen scissors) and flattening the bird. There are YouTube videos if you are unsure how to do this, or ask your butcher.

In a food processor, blitz all the marinade ingredients, except the onions, and with salt to taste, until smooth.

In a baking tray that you will use for roasting, pour the marinade over the chicken and rub all over. Leave to marinate for at least 1 hour or overnight in the fridge, covered with foil.

Bring your chicken to room temperature if refrigerated (it will take about an hour). Preheat the oven to 190°C/375°F/gas mark 5.

Remove the foil, sprinkle over the sliced onions and cover in foil again. Roast in the oven for 45 minutes. Meanwhile, wash your rice twice until the water runs clear, and set aside.

Remove the baking tray from the oven, lift out the chicken and add the rice, cardamom, cinnamon, saffron and turmeric to the baking tray. Give everything a stir to coat the rice, then add the water with salt to taste. Place the chicken on top, then roast, covered, for a further 30 minutes, removing the foil for the last 10 minutes to brown the skin.

Once the rice has absorbed the liquid and the chicken is cooked and browned, garnish with coriander, and pomegranate seeds if you like. Serve with poppadoms and lime-pickle-swirled yogurt. Carve at the table and let everyone help themselves.

butter chicken sphere

I often make this for my private clients, as it's a showstopper in terms of appearance and taste. In fact it's Joe Wicks's favourite! It really is the epitome of a dinner-party dish with a wow factor. It's a little bit more effort and challenging compared with the other recipes in this book, but the rewards are worth it. You can split up the process by making the sauce, filling and potato mash on day one, and doing the rest on day two. Or even batch-cook and freeze for future dinner parties!

A little background for context. Every world cuisine has a famous hero dish; India has butter chicken, more traditionally known as murgh makhani. Sharing similar traits as chicken tikka masala, which in fact was invented by the British, butter chicken is a celebration dish. My wedding feast wouldn't have been complete without it!

This sphere was born out of my love for makhani sauce. In an accidental combination of a hangover, leftover mince koftas and butter chicken, I made myself a plate of both elements and realized how delicious the crispy croquette tasted against the velvety creamy sauce. Never again will I dunk my mince croquettes (known as chops) into tomato ketchup!

Makes 4

For the chicken or paneer filling
2 tbsp rapeseed (canola) oil
2 cinnamon sticks
5 green cardamom pods
5 cloves
1 large onion, finely diced
2 tbsp ginger and garlic paste (see page 180 for homemade)
2 green finger chillies, finely chopped
250g (9oz) chicken thigh mince (ground chicken) or grated paneer (use shredded jackfruit for vegan)
1 tsp ground turmeric
½ tbsp ground coriander
½ tbsp ground cumin
½ tsp freshly ground black pepper
1 tbsp sea salt
75g (2½oz) frozen peas
Juice of ½ lemon
Large handful of chopped coriander (cilantro)

For the filling, heat the oil in a pan over a medium heat, then add the cinnamon, cardamom and cloves and cook for about 30 seconds, until sizzling. Add the onion and sauté for 7 minutes until golden, then add the ginger and garlic paste and chilli and sauté for 1 minute. Next, add the chicken mince (or paneer or jackfruit) and mix well, breaking down the bigger clumps of mince with a wooden spoon. Once fully cooked and evenly broken down, add the ground spices, salt and peas, and let this cook out for 10 minutes. Squeeze over the lemon and stir through the chopped coriander. Leave to cool.

Meanwhile, boil the potatoes whole in their skins for about 30 minutes until cooked through. Once cool enough to handle, grate them into a bowl. Add the milk and seasoning and mash, then beat until smooth. Set aside.

{ingredients and method continue overleaf...}

{continued...}

For the potato mash
3 medium Maris Piper potatoes
2 tbsp milk
Sea salt and ground pepper, to taste

For the makhani sauce
2 tbsp ghee
7 green cardamom pods, lightly crushed
2 black cardamom pods
2 bay leaves
5 cloves
1 cinnamon stick or cassia bark
4 tbsp ginger and garlic paste (see page
   180 for homemade)
1 tsp chopped green finger chilli
1 tbsp tomato purée (paste)
1½ tbsp ground coriander
1½ tbsp ground cumin
1 tsp ground turmeric
1 tsp Kashmiri chilli powder, or to taste
50ml (2fl oz) water
200g (7oz) plum tomatoes, blitzed
1 tsp garam masala
1 tbsp dried fenugreek leaves
   (kasoori methi)
1 tsp caster (superfine) sugar
150ml (5fl oz) double (heavy) cream
Squeeze of lemon juice
35g (1¼oz) unsalted butter

For the breadcrumb coating
50g (1¾oz) plain (all-purpose)
   flour, seasoned
2 eggs, beaten and seasoned
150g (5¼oz) panko breadcrumbs

Vegetable oil, for frying

For the makhani sauce, heat the ghee in a pan over a low–medium heat until fully melted, then add the whole spices and let them fizz for about 45 seconds. Now add the ginger and garlic paste and chilli, stirring for a minute to make sure it doesn't catch. Add the tomato purée followed by the ground spices except the garam masala and fenugreek leaves. Cook out for 1 minute then add the water and blitzed tomatoes. Now add garam masala and rub the fenugreek leaves between your palms over the sauce.

Simmer for about 12 minutes until the oil floats to the top – this is a sign the spices have cooked out. Remove the whole spices and blend the sauce until smooth. Season with salt, add the sugar, cream and lemon juice and stir continuously until the sauce is smooth. Taste and adjust the seasoning. Finish by adding the butter to achieve shine and a luxuriously smooth texture.

Between 2 sheets of cling film, roll out 1 tablespoon of potato mash to create a flat surface the size of a postcard. Now peel away the top layer of cling film and place 3 tablespoons of chicken (or paneer or jackfruit) filling. Now bring up each corner of the cling film and twist into a ball shape. Continue in the same fashion until all the mixture has been used up. Refrigerate for an hour to rest and set.

Meanwhile, prepare your breadcrumbing station. Put the flour, beaten egg and breadcrumbs in 3 separate bowls. Dip each sphere first in the flour, then the egg and then the panko. Once they are all coated, rest in the fridge for a further 30 minutes.

Heat enough vegetable oil to come halfway up the sides of a large, heavy-based saucepan or deep-fat fryer, and place over a medium heat until it reads 180°C (356°F) on a cooking thermometer, or a small piece of bread dropped into the oil turns golden brown in 45 seconds. In batches, deep-fry the spheres for 2–3 minutes, turning a few times to ensure even browning. Remove to kitchen paper to drain. If frying in advance, keep them warm in a low oven.

To serve, heat the makhani sauce, spoon about 2 tablespoons onto the middle of each plate and carefully place a sphere on top. Garnish with micro herbs and serve with salad.

thai sea bass parcels with coconut rice & asian slaw

Fish wrapped in banana leaves is a very common dish eaten all over Thailand. I remember sitting on the streets on a humid evening, unwrapping a banana leaf and enjoying this meal with an ice-cold beer in Koh Samui. I was inspired to make this holiday memory on a balmy summer evening in the UK. It was delicious on the BBQ but for all-year-round appeal, this roasted version is just as good. If you can get hold of banana leaves, it makes the presentation all the more beautiful.

Serves 6

6 sea bass fillets
6 banana leaves (optional)

For the marinade
3 tbsp coconut milk (use the top settled
  cream from a can of coconut milk)
2 tbsp Thai green curry paste
2 lemongrass stalks, finely chopped
1 tbsp ginger paste
1 tbsp garlic paste
1 tbsp fish sauce
1 tsp palm sugar
Sea salt, to taste

For the Asian slaw
1 large carrot, julienned
½ cucumber, julienned (remove the
  watery centre)
8 radishes, cut into sticks
Mango or pomelo, peeled and sliced
  (optional)
Handful of roasted peanuts
Handful of herbs, such as coriander
  (cilantro), mint and Thai basil,
  roughly chopped
1 quantity of nuoc cham dressing
  (see page 180)

To serve
Fragrant coconut rice (see page 185)
Lime wedges

In a large tray, mix all the marinade ingredients together. Add the sea bass fillets and coat them generously, then leave to marinate in the fridge for at least 2 hours, ideally overnight.

When ready to serve, preheat the oven to 200°C/400°F/gas mark 6.

Wrap each fillet in a banana leaf (or baking parchment if you can't find banana leaves), tying each up with kitchen twine like a present, and roast for 15 minutes.

Place all your slaw ingredients in a bowl, except the nuoc cham dressing, and dress at the table. Do not pour it over too early, so the slaw stays crisp.

Serve everything on banana leaves (if using), for that authentic Thai beach feel, with coconut rice and a big wedge of lime to squeeze over.

english breakfast parathas

This is my most memorable MasterChef dish. The challenge was to re-invent the iconic English breakfast, and I was on dangerous territory as there was huge pressure not to mess up a British institution! I thought about what Indian people have for breakfast and then decided to blend both cultures. After all, I am a British-Asian hybrid! In the words of Amol Rajan, 'Nisha, that was a gastronomic triumph'. That validation gave me the confidence to start developing my own unique creations.

Serves 6

For the paratha dough
400g (14oz) chapati flour, plus extra
    for dusting
1 tsp sea salt
1 tsp ajwain (carom) seeds
5 tsp vegetable oil
225ml (7¾fl oz) water
1 tbsp ghee or melted butter

For the paratha stuffing
6 Cumberland pork sausages (use
    chicken or plant-based if you prefer)
2 garlic cloves, crushed
1 tsp cumin seeds
1 green finger chilli, finely chopped
1 tsp ground cumin
1 tsp ground coriander
½ tsp ground turmeric
½ tsp garam masala

For the poached eggs
Olive oil, for brushing
Handful of coriander (cilantro) leaves
6 large eggs
Slices of red chilli
Sea salt and ground pepper, to taste

For the bacon jam (optional)
8 slices of smoked bacon
3 tbsp mango chutney

In a bowl, mix together the flour, salt, ajwain seeds, oil and water to make a smooth dough. Cover and rest for at least 15 minutes.

To make the bacon jam (if using), cook the bacon until crisp, then once cooled, blitz with the mango chutney in a small food processor. Set aside.

In a wide bowl, remove the skin from the sausages and gently mash the sausagemeat, then add the garlic and all the spices and mix to combine.

Divide the dough into 6 balls. Take a ball of dough and roll it out to about 8cm (3¼ inches) in diameter. Take a heaped tablespoon of filling, shape into a ball and place into the centre of the dough. Bring up all the edges to cover the stuffing and meet in the middle, breaking off any excess. Press down to flatten slightly, then place join-side down on a surface lightly dusted with flour. Roll out gently to a 12cm (4¾-inch) diameter disc. Repeat with the remaining dough and filling.

Place a heavy-based frying pan over a medium-high heat. Add a paratha and cook for about 3 minutes on one side, then flip over and repeat on the other side, pressing down with a spatula. When both sides become dry and start to colour, remove from the pan and brush with a little ghee or melted butter to get an even colour. Keep each paratha warm while you cook the rest, loosely wrapped in foil.

Now prep your eggs and set aside until you are ready to poach. Get 4 sheets of cling film (plastic wrap), approximately 40 x 40cm (16 x 16 inches), brush some olive oil over it and scatter over a few coriander leaves and a couple of slices of red chilli. Crack an egg in the centre of the cling film, sprinkle with salt and pepper and carefully bring up all the edges, gently squeezing out any air around the egg. Twist, then tie a knot in the cling

film to secure the egg snugly inside. Repeat with the remaining eggs. You can leave these in a bowl until ready to cook. Poach the egg parcels in a pan of simmering water for 5–6 minutes for soft poached eggs, or longer, until cooked to your liking.

When ready to plate, reheat the parathas in the oven if necessary, still wrapped in the foil. Place an egg on top of each paratha, with the bacon jam served alongside, if you like.

nduja scallops with silky corn & nori

This dish was inspired by a traditional Portuguese dish of spicy sausage, clams and coriander. Instead of a broth, I make creamy, sweetcorn purée which balances out the spicy notes of nduja. The freshness alongside the plump scallops makes the dish sing in harmony. A little fun touch with the popcorn adds crunch, but it's not totally necessary.

Feel free to use prawns (shrimp) if you can't get hold of scallops. Serve on a large platter or individual plates for a beautiful starter for your dinner party.

Serves 4

12 fresh scallops, cleaned
2 tbsp nduja paste
1 tsp olive oil
Splash (about 3 tbsp) of white or rosé wine
25g (1oz) butter
Sea salt and ground pepper, to taste

For the sweetcorn purée
700g (1lb 8½oz) drained canned or frozen sweetcorn
100ml (3½fl oz) chicken or vegetable stock
50ml (2fl oz) double (heavy) cream
½ tsp dried oregano
Small knob of salted butter

To garnish
Coriander (cilantro) cress or leaves
1 nori sheet, cut into strips (optional)
1 lime, for squeezing over
Small handful of salted popcorn (optional)

Rub the scallops with the nduja paste and olive oil and set aside for them to marinate. The scallops should be at room temperature before cooking.

Prepare the sweetcorn purée by simmering the corn in the stock for 10 minutes over a low heat. Add the cream and oregano, then transfer to a blender and blitz until smooth. Strain through a sieve (strainer) to catch all the husks. Add the butter and season to taste. The purée should be smooth and creamy and can be reheated gently when ready to serve.

Place a large non-stick frying pan over a medium-high heat. Once hot, add the scallops, ensuring they are not touching each other. Sear for 2 minutes, pressing down on them with a spatula until the underside has good caramelization. Flip over and cook for a further 2 minutes on the other side. It's important not to overcook scallops or they turn chewy. Add the splash of wine to deglaze the pan, then add the butter and take off the heat.

Now plate up on a large platter to share, or individual plates for a starter. Spoon on the sweetcorn purée, arrange the scallops on top and drizzle over any nduja butter from the pan. Sprinkle over coriander cress or leaves and nori strips (if using), a squeeze of lime juice and a few popcorn kernels if you like. Soak up the joy from your guests when this is served.

turkish eggs with potato latkes

I don't think there's anything wrong with having breakfast dishes for dinner, or having evening meals in the morning. So here is this beautiful brunch dish that you should serve for a dinner party, because sometimes breaking the rules keeps life interesting! I've added potato latkes to make this extra-special, but you can just serve the eggs with toasted sourdough bread. You can make a lot of the elements ahead of time and just reheat once your guests arrive. It is truly delicious and addictive – easy to see why it was one of my best sellers when I had my café.

Serves 4

8 eggs
Oil, for greasing and frying
Small handful of mint leaves,
    finely sliced
Sea salt, to taste

For the latkes
3 large Maris Piper potatoes (about
    600g/1lb 5oz in total)
1 onion, finely sliced
4 tbsp plain (all-purpose) flour (or
    gram/chickpea flour for gluten-free)
1 egg

For the yogurt sauce
500g (1lb 2oz) Greek yogurt
1 garlic clove, crushed

For the chilli butter
50g (1¾oz) salted butter
15g (½oz) Aleppo pepper (or regular
    chilli flakes with a pinch of paprika)

Crack each egg into a piece of oiled cling film (plastic wrap), about 30 x 30cm (12 x 12 inches), bringing up each corner, squeezing out the air and tying a knot in the middle. This can be done in advance so you don't have the panic of poached eggs when your guests arrive, and they are guaranteed to be perfect!

Mix the yogurt and garlic for the sauce, adding salt to taste.

Scrub the potatoes clean and coarsely grate (skin on). Place in a clean tea (dish) towel or muslin (cheesecloth) with the onion, and squeeze out all the excess water. Tip into a bowl and add the flour, egg and some salt to taste. Mix well.

Cover the base of a large frying pan with oil and place over a medium heat. Shape little golf-ball-sized portions of potato mixture and flatten. Gently place in the oil and fry on each side for 2 minutes until crisp and golden. Drain on kitchen paper. If you're making ahead, reheat in the oven when ready to serve.

Once you're ready to plate up, drop the cling film eggs parcels into a pan of boiling water and cook for 5 minutes for a runny yolk, or 8 minutes for hard-boiled.

Meanwhile, melt the butter in a pan until foaming and slightly brown, and add the Aleppo pepper.

To assemble, take 2 heaped tablespoons of the garlic yogurt and swirl it onto the bottom of each plate. Arrange 3 latkes and 2 poached eggs on top, drizzle over the chilli butter and garnish with sliced mint.

masala plates

Entertaining is never more effortless than when you embrace the philosophy of one-pot wonders and clever traybakes. A bountiful curry poured over rice, a whole roast chicken ready for carving or maybe a help-yourself-style spread. This section is full of abundance and ease, with masala at its core.

Many of these techniques have been inherited from my mum and aunties. I remember Mum cooking for ten when only four people were coming round. Tactfully done to ensure you had plenty, but also purposefully to pack leftovers for the guests as a gift. Mum would forcefully encourage me to stay in the kitchen to watch what she was doing, asking me to do tedious tasks like picking the leaves from the coriander stalks or podding peas. I now realize it was just her way of keeping me in the kitchen to absorb the ritual of what she was doing. I've subconsciously learned how to host and cook for a crowd because I watched my mum doing it growing up. She always used to say, 'I know you would rather watch TV, but you must learn this; one day it will come in useful.' And she was right.

Under the stairs or in the garage would be the big aluminium pots with no handles saved for the mass cooking marathon. Mum made bulk cooking look so easy; everything was ready hours before guests arrived, simply needing to be heated up, even though guests would insist on 'helping' with the cooking. It was always jovial banter and Mum would usher them away to sit and drink more, and nibble on homemade Bombay mix.

These make-ahead dishes will intensify in flavour, and marinating or cooking some of the recipes the night before will reward you with even more taste. This section will take you to faraway places. Masala concoctions from the Indian, Malay and Thai subcontinents will fill your kitchen with heady aromas, and your guests with joyful anticipation, probably hoping there is enough in the pot to take home for breakfast!

red thai daal with coconut sambal

Daal is a store-cupboard saviour. Dried lentils waiting to be plumped up and drizzled with flavour; the ultimate comfort food. Humble yet elegant, a bowl of daal is a love letter for the soul.

Here's a hack to a flavourful daal with minimal ingredients: a shop-bought Thai paste has ginger, garlic, chilli, lemongrass and more, which saves you buying and chopping lots of herbs and spices.

Make the optional coconut sambal if you fancy, but otherwise a bowl of this Thai-inspired daal mopped up with paratha or rice is enough.

Serves 4

1 tbsp coconut (or rapeseed) oil
1 onion, finely chopped
1 x 400g (14oz) can of coconut milk
1 tbsp red curry paste
½ tsp ground turmeric
1 tsp sea salt
250g (9oz) red lentils (or any you
  have; just adjust the cooking times
  accordingly)
400ml (14fl oz) water

For the coconut sambal (optional)
80g (3oz) desiccated (dried shredded)
  coconut
1 green finger chilli
1 garlic clove, peeled
25g (1oz) coriander (cilantro)
Juice of 1 lime
Pinch of sea salt

To serve (optional)
Fresh curry leaves, fried until crisp in
  coconut oil
Chilli oil (see page 179 for homemade)

Heat the oil in a medium saucepan over a medium-hot heat, add the onion and cook for 4–5 minutes to brown slightly, then add 1 tablespoon of the coconut cream from the top of the coconut milk can, along with the curry paste. Mix well, then add the turmeric, salt, lentils, the rest of the coconut milk and the water (you can measure the water by filling the empty coconut milk can). Bring to the boil, then cover and simmer over a gentle heat for 25 minutes.

Meanwhile, in a food processor, blitz together all the ingredients for the coconut sambal (if using).

Taste for seasoning and serve in bowls, topped with the coconut sambal and curry leaves, and chilli oil, if you like. The daal and sambal keep well in the fridge for 3 days, so this is a great one to make ahead of your dinner party.

thai basil chicken

I'm sitting under a bamboo beach shack, tiny and family-run on a hot balmy evening in Koh Samui. They are bringing out plate after plate of this mince dish onto everyone's table. I lean over and ask what the dish is called, and they proudly announce: 'Pad krapow gai.' And ever since then, when I make this dish it reminds of 'The Hut' in the fishermen's village.

It dawned on me that nearly all cultures have a signature mince dish. There's chilli con carne, spaghetti bolognese and Indian lamb kheema. This is the Thai version of a chilli with rice, utterly comforting, familiar yet totally distinct with its flavour of aniseedy Thai basil. An easy crowd pleaser for your next dinner party.

Serves 4

2½ tbsp coconut or vegetable oil, plus a little extra for the eggs, if serving
150g (5¼oz) green beans, cut in half
1 medium onion, diced
3cm (1¼-inch) piece of fresh ginger, peeled and grated
7 garlic cloves, crushed
2 red bird's eye chillies, finely sliced, plus extra (optional) to serve
1 lemongrass stalk, outer leaves removed, bashed and finely chopped
600g (1lb 5oz) chicken mince (ground chicken), or any of your choice, such as pork or soya
1 tbsp light soy sauce
2 tbsp dark soy sauce
1 tbsp oyster sauce (or vegan mushroom sauce)
1 tbsp fish sauce (or vegan version)
1 tbsp brown sugar
1 bunch (25g/1oz) of Thai basil (not to be confused with holy basil), leaves only
4 eggs (optional)

To serve
Fragrant coconut rice (page 185)
Lime wedges

Heat 1 tablespoon of the oil in a pan over a medium-high heat, add the green beans and cook for 3–4 minutes, trying not to stir too much so you get some nice charring. Remove from the pan and set aside. Add the remaining oil to the same pan and sauté the onion until translucent. Next, add the ginger, garlic, chilli and lemongrass and cook out for 2 minutes. Tip in your mince and break it up with a wooden spoon. Cook, stirring, until browned, then add all the sauces and the sugar. To make it easier, have the sauces mixed together in a small bowl and tip it all in at the same time.

Return the beans to the pan, scatter in most of the Thai basil leaves (save a few to garnish) and mix in. You can make it up to this point ahead of time, and reheat.

If serving with eggs, fry them in a little oil in a frying pan. To assemble, serve the chicken on top of coconut rice, with an egg on top, if using, garnished with the reserved Thai basil leaves and red chilli, if liked, and a squeeze of lime.

portuguese lime & coconut chicken

Having family in Lisbon, I have grown up on authentic peri peri chicken and roadside grilled sardines. Chargrilled peri peri chicken is served with fresh crisps (not fries) in Lisbon. My suggestion would be to serve this with a big green salad and ready salted crisps (chips) in summer, but feel free to make potato wedges or fat chips (fries) in the colder months. The crisps actually emphasize the softness of the chicken, and the contrast is extraordinary.

This recipe works beautifully on the BBQ (grill), is great with the salad on page 118 or the whole roast cauliflower on page 61. This is a simple dinner-party dish you will be able to whip up with minimum ingredients, and one you will make on repeat!

Serves 4

8 bone-in, skin-on chicken thighs
2 tbsp extra virgin olive oil
8 garlic cloves, crushed
2 tbsp Korean gochugaru chilli flakes (or regular chilli flakes)
2 tbsp desiccated (dried shredded) coconut
2 tbsp maple syrup (or honey)
Grated zest and juice of 2 limes
Handful of coriander (cilantro) stalks, finely chopped
Sea salt and ground pepper, to taste

Preheat the oven to 200°C/400°F/gas mark 6.

Make a couple of slits in each chicken thigh and place skin-side up in a baking tray. Simply mix all the remaining ingredients together, pour over the chicken, then roast in the oven for 40 minutes until the skin is crispy.

That's it – delicious simplicity.

goan salmon curry

I thought I was being sent home at this stage on MasterChef. It was only my second time back in that scary kitchen and I had the ludicrous task of cooking 8 plates of food, 2 courses in 1 hour and 15 minutes AND for previous MasterChef winners! I made a lamb curry puff and chutney to start, and this Goan salmon curry with cumin rice for main. Since I felt so rushed, I convinced myself I was out, but this was one of my strongest rounds! I sailed into the quarter finals, despite John Torode doubting if rich oily salmon would work in an Indian curry. Since then, I've had hundreds of requests for this recipe, so here it is. A beautiful orange-hued curry with the seal of approval from John Torode and Gregg Wallace. To quote John: '*This is a crescendo of flavour, layers and layers of depth*'.

Serves 4

3 tbsp coconut oil (or a flavourless oil such as rapeseed/canola)
7 each of green cardamom pods, cloves and black peppercorns
1 cinnamon stick
1 tsp fennel seeds
2 large onions, finely diced
2 tbsp ginger and garlic paste (see page 180 for homemade)
2 green finger chillies, finely chopped
2 tbsp ground coriander
2 tbsp ground cumin
1 tsp ground turmeric
1 tsp Kashmiri chilli powder
1 tsp garam masala
1 x 400g (14oz) can of good-quality plum tomatoes, blitzed, or 400ml (14fl oz) passata (sieved tomatoes)
Handful of coriander (cilantro), finely chopped (save the leaves to finish)
200ml (7fl oz) coconut milk
1 tbsp tamarind paste or ½ tsp tamarind concentrate
4 skinless salmon fillets (each about 120g/4oz), cubed
Sea salt, to taste

To finish and serve
Reserved coriander (cilantro) leaves, finely chopped
1 lemon, for squeezing
Cardamom and cumin rice (page 185)
Chapatis (page 176)
Kachumber (page 184)

In a wide, shallow pan, gently heat the oil over a low heat and add the cardamom, cloves, peppercorns, cinnamon stick and fennel seeds. When you sizzle whole spices in oil like this you are infusing the oil for that first base layer of flavour. A good curry should have layers of spices so you get complexities and the curry doesn't just taste of one spice.

Next, add the onions and spend at least 10–15 minutes gently caramelizing them over a low heat, being careful not to burn them. Spending time caramelizing at this stage gives the curry a beautiful natural sweetness, so this is very important. Now tip in the ginger and garlic paste, and green chillies, stirring away the rawness for 1 minute, before adding all the ground spices. Tip in the tomatoes or passata, and the coriander stalks, and simmer for about 10 minutes until you see oil rising to the surface. This is an indication that the spices have cooked out.

This stage is optional but will give more flavour: remove the cinnamon stick and the seeds from the cardamom pods, discarding the husks and returning the seeds to the dish. Using a stick blender, blitz to a smooth paste.

Add the coconut milk and tamarind and stir them in, then check the seasoning and add salt to taste. Gently arrange the salmon cubes in the sauce and ensure each piece is covered. Cover and cook over a very low heat for 15 minutes, trying not to agitate the salmon too much to prevent it all falling apart. Once cooked, finish with the coriander and lots of lemon juice. Serve with cardamom and cumin rice, chapatis and kachumber.

coconut saag paneer with peas

It was only when I started doing my dinner parties that I discovered how much everyone loved saag paneer (especially Ellie Goulding!). Paneer is often regarded as a celebratory ingredient, and pairing it with creamy spinach makes it even more dreamy. I have no idea why it's just a side dish in restaurants; I even had it on my wedding day menu.

I've added peas to this version because I love the way they add sweetness. Serve with chapatis, naan or steamed basmati rice with poppadoms and salad for a dinner-party feast. No one will miss the meat, but having said that, this works equally well with chicken pieces. I usually make this with frozen spinach for convenience and to keep it budget-friendly. However, by all means use fresh if you prefer. It's a perfect make-ahead dish, too.

(Disclaimer for the purists out there, saag is a north Indian term which refers to a mix of mustard greens, spinach and other greens as a combination. Palak means spinach only; however, most restaurants will refer to this dish as saag paneer, so for the sake of familiarity, I'm using the more common description!)

Serves 4

4 tbsp coconut oil or ghee
1 tsp cumin seeds
1 cinnamon stick
1 large onion, diced
2 tbsp ginger and garlic paste (see page 180 for homemade)
2 green finger chillies finely chopped
1 tomato, diced
1 tsp ground turmeric
1 tbsp ground cumin
1 tbsp ground coriander
½ tsp garam masala
½–1 tsp hot chilli powder
1 tsp dried fenugreek leaves (kasoori methi)
450g (1lb) frozen chopped spinach, thawed (700g/1lb 8½oz fresh)
350g (12oz) paneer, cut into 2cm (¾-inch) cubes
75ml (5 tbsp) coconut milk (mainly fat solids)
50g (1¾oz) frozen petits pois
Squeeze of lemon juice
Small knob of butter (optional)
Sea salt, to taste

Heat half the coconut oil or ghee (or oil if you prefer) in a pan over a medium-low heat, add the cumin seeds and cinnamon stick and cook until they fizz, then add the onion. Stir-fry for about 5 minutes until slightly brown, then add the ginger and garlic paste with the green chillies and sauté for a minute or so.

Add the tomato and all the ground spices, fenugreek leaves, and salt to taste. Add a splash of water if needed, followed by the spinach. Stir to combine and let the mixture simmer for 10 minutes.

Meanwhile, heat the remaining coconut oil or ghee in a large non-stick frying pan. Add the cubed paneer, avoid stirring too much, and let each side catch some colour before gently flipping each cube. This should take about 3–4 minutes.

Remove the cinnamon stick from the spinach mixture and purée slightly with a stick blender until smooth, but still with some texture. Add the coconut milk and tumble in the paneer cubes and peas. Simmer for 10 minutes. Finish with a squeeze of lemon, and a knob of butter, if you like.

sri lankan beetroot curry

My earliest memory of eating beetroot is in Pizza Hut! In the 1980s, going
to Pizza Hut was a big deal, and the highlight wasn't even the pizza – it
was the salad bar! A help-yourself buffet of salad but you couldn't go back
for more, so everyone had a technique of filling it as high as possible. I used
to build a cucumber wall, with a foundation of potato salad, then pile on
tiny purple beetroot cubes, not only because it made the potatoes pink but
because it was delicious. No one else could understand why a six-year-old
loved beetroot!

Anyway, long story short: here is a curry with only beetroot, and I love it!
This is a beautiful side dish and I'll always make it whenever I have fresh
beetroot to hand. It's perfect with any meat curry or another veg curry
on the side, a humble staple in Sri Lanka which I first experienced
in the Maldives cooked by Sri Lankan chefs, because the islands are
only 4 hours apart.

Serves 2 as a main, 4 as a side

1 tbsp coconut oil
1 tsp mustard seeds
20 fresh curry leaves
1 small red onion, sliced
2 green finger chillies, finely chopped
1 tbsp ginger and garlic paste (see page
    180 for homemade)
½ tsp ground turmeric
1 tsp medium curry powder (ideally
    Sri Lankan)
3 raw beetroots (beets), peeled and
    grated
½ tsp Kashmiri chilli powder
1 x 400g (14oz) can of coconut milk,
    top creamy part only (add the rest of
    the coconut milk to smoothies)
Sea salt, to taste
Handful of coriander (cilantro), finely
    chopped, to garnish

Heat the coconut oil in a pan over a medium heat, add the
mustard seeds and cook until they splutter, then take off the heat
and add the curry leaves. These will crackle and spit too. Add the
onion and green chillies, place back over the heat and cook out
for 5–7 minutes until softened.

Next, tip in the ginger and garlic paste, turmeric and curry
powder. Sauté for about a minute, before adding the grated
beetroot and combining it with the spices by mixing well. Add
the chilli powder, coconut cream, and salt to taste. Cover and
cook for 10 minutes over a low heat. Check the beetroot is
softened and serve with a garnish of fresh coriander.

ganesh's butter chicken

This is going to sound crazy, but one of my best butter chicken memories is from Vietnam! Confession: I haven't been to Delhi so I cannot compare with one from the birthplace of murgh makhani (butter chicken). I asked the chef why his was so good and he told me a lot of the spices are grown in Vietnam. If you find yourself in Hoi An, please go to Ganesh; it will be one of the best meals of your life. I tried to get their recipe, without success, but this is the closest I've got to recreating that flavour, and if there was ever a dinner-party-worthy curry, it has to be the magnificent butter chicken. You can replace the chicken with 400g (14oz) of paneer.

Serves 4

10 boneless, skinless chicken thighs
 (about 1kg/2lb 3oz in total), cut into
 large pieces
Naan (page 175) or steamed rice, to serve

For the marinade
3 tbsp Greek yogurt
3 level tsp ginger & garlic paste
 (see page 180 for homemade)
1 tbsp ground turmeric
2 tbsp Kashmiri chilli powder
Juice of 1 lemon
Sea salt, to taste

For the sauce
2 tbsp ghee (or 3 tbsp oil)
1 cinnamon stick
7 green cardamom pods
3 black cardamom pods
7 cloves
1 bay leaf (optional)
3 tbsp ginger and garlic paste (see page
 180 for homemade)
1 green finger chilli, finely chopped
1 tbsp ground cumin
1 tbsp ground coriander
1 tbsp Kashmiri chilli powder
1 tbsp tomato purée (paste)
½ x 400g (14oz) can of plum
 tomatoes, blitzed
75ml (5 tbsp) water
150ml (5fl oz) double (heavy) cream,
 plus a little extra to drizzle
1 tbsp dried fenugreek leaves (kasoori
 methi), plus extra to finish
1 tsp garam masala
1 tbsp sugar (or honey)
25g (1oz) butter

This recipe is a two-part process. Start by combining the chicken with the marinade ingredients in a bowl. Cover and marinate, ideally overnight in the fridge, but for at least 1 hour.

Preheat the oven to 200°C/400°F/gas mark 6.

Ensuring the chicken isn't fridge-cold, skewer the pieces onto wooden or metal skewers and place over a baking tray. Roast in the oven for 45 minutes until the chicken is cooked and you have some charring (this method mimics a tandoor, the traditional way to cook butter chicken).

While the chicken is roasting, make the velvety sauce. Melt the ghee or oil in a large, wide pan over a medium-low heat. Add the whole spices and bay leaf (if using), to flavour the oil and, once fizzing, add the ginger and garlic paste and green chilli. Cook this out for about 2 minutes, ensuring it doesn't take on any colour. Tip in the ground cumin and coriander and the Kashmiri chilli powder. Add the tomato purée to cook out with the spices for about a minute, then tip in the blitzed tomatoes and water.

Let this simmer for at least 10 minutes until the oil has separated from the sauce. Now add the cream, fenugreek leaves, garam masala, sugar (or honey) and salt to taste.

Once the chicken is cooked, remove from the skewers and transfer it all into the sauce with the liquid that has accumulated in the tray. Stir everything together, and finish the dish with the chunk of butter, a sprinkling of fenugreek leaves and a drizzle of cream. Check for seasoning and ensure there is a level of sweetness. Butter chicken does not require coriander leaves but feel free to add. Serve with the naans or some steamed rice.

alleppey houseboat mushroom curry

Everyone's bucket list should include a houseboat stay in the Keralan backwaters. Here you will find the freshest, most authentic food while wrapped in the beauty of the tranquil surroundings. Every houseboat will have a chef with his home recipe to delight you. Most boats have fish curries as standard, and I've taken the inspiration from these flavours to make a vegan version; the meaty texture of oyster mushrooms does not disappoint! A great make-ahead dish that just requires reheating and pairs beautifully with the cumin rice on page 185.

Serves 2–3

3 tbsp sunflower oil
500g (1lb 2oz) king oyster mushrooms,
    sliced lengthways
1 tsp black mustard seeds
1 tsp fennel seeds
10 fresh curry leaves
1 large onion, finely chopped
1 tbsp ginger and garlic paste (see
    page 180 for homemade)
2 green finger chillies, sliced
1 tsp tomato purée (paste)
10 cherry tomatoes, halved
½ tsp ground turmeric
½ tsp Kashmiri chilli powder
1 tsp medium curry powder
1 tsp sea salt
1 x 400g (14oz) can of coconut milk
1 tsp mango chutney (optional)
Small bunch of coriander (cilantro),
    to garnish

To serve
Cardamom and cumin rice (page 185)
Lemon wedges

Heat 2 tablespoons of the oil in a pan over a high heat, add the mushrooms and stir-fry for about 4 minutes until browned, then remove from the pan and set aside.

Heat the remaining oil in the same pan, add the mustard and fennel seeds and cook until they sizzle, then add the curry leaves and onion. Sauté over a medium heat until the onion is translucent and slightly brown.

Now add the ginger and garlic paste and green chillies and stir-fry for 30 seconds, before adding the tomato purée, halved cherry tomatoes, ground spices and salt. Cook out for a minute, then add the coconut milk and simmer for 3 minutes. Add the mango chutney (if using), and return the mushrooms to the sauce.

Cover and cook for another 15 minutes or until the mushrooms are fully cooked through.

Garnish with coriander and serve with lemon rice, and lemon wedges for squeezing over.

langkawi chicken rendang

When I return from holiday I come home with two souvenirs: one is a
fridge magnet and the other is recipes scribbled down on napkins from
local chefs. This recipe was given to me by the head chef in our resort
in Langkawi, Malaysia. The only meal I'll typically eat at a hotel is the
magnificent breakfast, and at The Andaman, they served chicken rendang
with coconut rice. I devoured a bowl of this luscious rendang every
morning under swaying palm trees. I felt nourished and satisfied; it's a
great balance of protein with the right amount of spice. It's the perfect
dish to make ahead of time, which intensifies in flavour. It is addictive
and worth all the effort... come with me to Langkawi!

Serves 4

For the rendang paste
5 shallots, peeled
2.5cm (1-inch) piece of galangal
3 lemongrass stalks, white part only
8 garlic cloves, peeled
5cm (2-inch) piece of fresh ginger
10–12 dried chillies, soaked in just-
    boiled water, then drained

For the base curry
5 tbsp cooking oil
1 cinnamon stick, about 5cm
    (2 inches) long
3 cloves
3 star anise
3 green cardamom pods
700g (1lb 8½oz) skinless chicken thighs,
    boned and chopped into large chunks
    (keep some bone-in for extra flavour
    if you like)
1 lemongrass stalk, cut into 10cm
    (4-inch) lengths and pounded
1 x 400g (14oz) can of coconut milk
2 tsp tamarind paste
100ml (3½fl oz) water
6 fresh makrut lime leaves, stacked up,
    rolled and very finely sliced
4 tbsp kerisik (toasted desiccated/dry
    shredded coconut)
1 tsp garam masala
1 tbsp sugar/palm sugar, or to taste
2 tsp sea salt, or to taste

To serve
Fragrant coconut rice (see page 185)
Pickled cucumbers

Preheat the oven to 200°C/400°F/gas mark 6.

Roughly chop the rendang paste ingredients then blend together
in a food processor until fine, adding a splash of water if needed.

Heat the oil in an ovenproof pot with a lid (ideally cast-iron)
over a medium heat, then add the cinnamon, cloves, star anise
and cardamom and cook until sizzling. Add the spice paste and
stir-fry for about 3 minutes, until aromatic. Add the chicken and
lemongrass and stir for 1 minute, then add the coconut milk,
tamarind and water, and simmer over a medium heat, stirring
frequently, for about 15 minutes.

Add the lime leaves, kerisik, garam masala, sugar and salt to the
chicken pot, stirring to blend well with the chicken. Cover with
a lid and pop in the oven for 1½ hours, or until the chicken is
really tender and the gravy has dried up. You can also do this on
the stovetop if you prefer.

Leave to stand for 30 minutes before serving. It will come out of
the oven piping hot, and you want it to be a nice temperature to
be able to appreciate the layers of flavour.

Serve with fragrant coconut rice and pickled cucumbers.

mombasa prawn masala

My father grew up on the Kenyan tropical island of Mombasa and food was his connection to childhood memories. If it wasn't for him I would have been vegetarian, as mum did all the cooking growing up and she is from Gujarat, a predominantly vegetarian state in north west India. I would only be exposed to meat and seafood in restaurants or my auntie's house, who was a chef for British Airways. My mum realized I was quite the foodie, so she began to experiment cooking with chicken, lamb and prawns.

It was this prawn curry that always got me super-excited. Prawns were an expensive luxury so it was only on special occasions like birthdays when we would enjoy this indulgence. In the 1980s you could only buy those tiny frozen prawns, usually precooked. My dad would reminisce about the fresh prawns from the beach market he would buy twice a year and spend hours cleaning them for this very same prawn curry.

I hope this becomes your special occasion dish too; your dinner guests are in for a treat.

Serves 4

5 tbsp rapeseed (canola) oil
5 green cardamom pods
1 cinnamon stick
8 black peppercorns
3 whole cloves
1 bay leaf
3 brown onions, finely chopped
8 fat garlic cloves, crushed
2 green finger chillies, finely chopped
1 tbsp tomato purée (paste)
1½ tbsp ground cumin
1½ tbsp ground coriander
1 tsp ground turmeric
1 tsp Kashmiri chilli powder
1 tsp garam masala
1 x 400g (14oz) can of plum
   tomatoes, blitzed
700g (1lb 8½oz) frozen prawns
   (shrimp), ideally tail-on, thawed
100ml (3½fl oz) water
1 tsp oyster sauce (optional)
1 tsp dark soy sauce (optional)
Handful of coriander (cilantro), leaves and
   stalks separated and finely chopped
Sea salt and lemon juice, to taste
Chapatis (page 176), naan (page 175) or
   steamed rice, to serve

Heat the oil in a large stainless steel pot over a medium heat and add the cardamom, cinnamon, peppercorns, cloves and bay leaf. Let them sizzle so the oil is infused with the first layer of flavour. Next, add the onions and spend at least 15 minutes caramelizing them until they are deep golden brown but not burnt. Now add the garlic and green chillies and sauté for about 1 minute, before adding the tomato purée and all the ground spices and a pinch of salt. Gently cook out for about 1 minute then pour in the blitzed tomatoes. Stir, cover and cook for at least 15 minutes over a low heat until you see oil floating to the top. This means your ground spices have been cooked out.

Add your prawns, stir well, then add the water, oyster and soy sauces (if using), and chopped coriander stalks. Cover and cook for a further 15 minutes until the prawns are cooked and you have a rich gravy. Add a little more water if needed. Remove the whole spices, if you like, and garnish with the chopped coriander leaves and squeeze over some lemon juice.

Serve with chapatis, naan or steamed rice.

sri lankan chicken masala traybake

Using just one tray for a dinner party makes so much sense; a stress-free way to deliver a crowd pleaser, with minimum washing up. This is another recipe born out of a fridge raid to use up curry leaves and tomatoes on their last legs! Sri Lankan curries use coconut, curry leaves and a special roasted curry powder. Here I use a shortcut, but buy the best medium curry powder you can find. For ultimate perfection, I like to serve this with cardamom and cumin rice, naan, some kachumber and the coconut sambal on page 174 to make this totally restaurant-worthy! This is the perfect make-ahead dinner-party dish. You can marinate and keep the chicken and curry sauce for up to 2 days in the fridge, just bring it back up to room temperature before roasting. The rice, salad and sambal can also be made in advance.

Serves 4

10 bone-in, skin-on chicken thighs
3 tbsp rapeseed (canola) oil
3 shallots, sliced
30 fresh curry leaves

For the masala curry
2 tbsp rapeseed (canola) oil
5 garlic cloves, crushed
1 tsp ground turmeric
1 tbsp Kashmiri chilli powder
Juice of ½ lemon 3 ripe vine tomatoes
    (or 20 cherry tomatoes)
1 tbsp tomato purée (paste)
1 small onion, cut into chunks
20g (¾oz) fresh ginger, peeled and
    cut into chunks
2 tbsp medium curry powder
1 tsp palm sugar (or honey)
1 x 400g (14oz) can of coconut milk
1 tsp sea salt

To serve
Cardamom and cumin rice (page 185)
    or naan (page 175)
Beetroot curry (page 80)
Green coconut sambal (page 174),
    optional

In a food processor, blitz all the ingredients for the masala curry until smooth. Spread over the chicken thighs (in a non-metallic dish) and marinate for at least 2 hours, or ideally overnight, in the fridge.

Transfer the chicken and sauce to a baking tray and bring to room temperature. Preheat the oven to 200°C/400°F/gas mark 6.

Roast for 45–50 minutes until the skin has browned and the sauce has thickened. Remove and set aside to rest for 10 minutes.

Meanwhile, heat the oil in a frying pan over a medium-hot heat, add the shallots and fry for a couple of minutes until crispy, then add the curry leaves and leave to sizzle for a few seconds. Pour this over the chicken as a final garnish and serve with cumin and cardamom rice, beetroot curry and the coconut sambal, if you like.

delica pumpkin laksa

As the weather starts to change from summer to autumn, it's natural
to seek comfort and warmth from food, and my default setting for this
is laksa: a steaming hot bowl of spicy coconutty curry broth laced with
layers of flavour and noodles. With pumpkins and squashes in abundance
during the beginning of autumn, it makes sense to use the bounty of these
plump vegetables. This is another great crowd pleaser that can be prepped
in advance to be heated and assembled when your guests arrive. If you are
short of time or can't source the ingredients, then using a ready-made curry
paste in place of the laksa paste is a good hack.

Serves 4

2 tbsp cooking oil
600g (1lb 5oz) Delica squash or
    pumpkin, peeled, deseeded and cut
    into large cubes
2 x 400g (14oz) cans of coconut milk
2 tbsp light soy sauce
2 tbsp fish sauce
1 tbsp palm sugar or white sugar
500ml (17fl oz) vegetable stock
4 nests of rice noodles
250g (9oz) tofu (bean curd) puffs
    (optional; shop-bought is fine)

*For the laksa paste (or use shop-bought
red Thai curry paste)*
15 dried chillies, soaked in water
5 small Thai shallots
4 lemongrass stalks, outer leaves
    removed
8 garlic cloves, peeled
4cm (1½-inch) piece of galangal or
    fresh ginger, peeled
6 fresh makrut lime leaves, central
    stems removed
1 tbsp curry powder
1 tsp ground turmeric
Small bunch of coriander (cilantro)
    stalks (save the leaves for garnish)
1 tsp peanut butter or tahini (optional)

To garnish
Julienned cucumber
Coriander (cilantro) or Thai basil
Sliced red chilli
Spring onions (scallions), sliced
Beansprouts
Lime wedges

Preheat the oven to 200°C/400°F/gas mark 6.

Drizzle the oil over the pumpkin or squash chunks in a roasting
tray and roast in the oven for 40 minutes, until tender.

Meanwhile, if making your own paste, add all the ingredients to
a food processor and blitz to a smooth paste, adding a little water
if needed.

Add the coconut cream that has settled at the top of the coconut
milk cans to a large pot, with 1 teaspoon of laksa paste per
person, or to taste. Place over a gentle heat and cook out for
about 5 minutes. Now add the rest of the coconut milk, the soy
sauce, fish sauce, sugar and stock, and let everything simmer
for about 15 minutes.

At this point you can keep the broth ready until your guests
arrive and just reheat it before assembling your laksa bowls.

Soak your rice noodles for about 5 minutes in just-boiled water;
they only need hydrating, not cooking. Drain.

Now assemble your bowls: add the noodles first, followed by
2 ladles of broth, or enough to cover the noodles. Next, the
roasted pumpkin and tofu puffs (if using). Add garnishes of your
choice, squeeze over some lime juice and enjoy. A real wow-
factor bowl of food with a melody of sweet, spicy and sour notes.

lamb kofta masala (*mamra*)

This kofta (meatball) masala is a family favourite but also a dinner-party classic when I have lots of people coming round. Its flavours and textures mature with time, making it an ideal choice for preparing in advance. Serve with chapatis, rice, spaghetti, or even couscous with a kachumber salad.

Serves 4

For the meatballs
800g (1lb 12oz) minced (ground) lamb, at least 5% fat (turkey mince also works really well)
1 tbsp ginger and garlic paste (see page 180 for homemade)
1–2 green finger chillies, finely chopped
1 tsp ground cumin
1 tsp ground coriander
½ tsp ground turmeric
½ tsp garam masala
Small handful of finely chopped coriander (cilantro)
½ tsp salt
½ tsp pepper

For the masala gravy
5 tbsp vegetable oil
5 green cardamom pods
8 black peppercorns
3 whole cloves
1 cinnamon stick
1 bay leaf
3 brown onions, finely diced
8 fat garlic cloves, crushed
2 green finger chillies, finely chopped
1 tbsp tomato purée (paste)
1½ tbsp ground cumin
1½ tbsp ground coriander
1 tsp ground turmeric
1 tsp Kashmiri red chilli (only ½ tsp if you don't have Kashmiri)
1 tsp garam masala
½ tsp dried fenugreek leaves (kasoori methi)
1 x 400g (14oz) can of plum tomatoes, blitzed
Handful of coriander (cilantro), finely chopped
Sea salt and ground pepper, to taste
1 lemon, cut into wedges, to serve

In a large bowl, mix together all the ingredients for the meatballs by hand, kneading gently until incorporated (never over-mix ground meat, as it will become tough). Shape the mixture into mini balls about 20g (¾oz) each, place on a tray and leave in the fridge while you make the gravy.

In a wide pan, heat the oil gently over a medium heat and add the cardamom pods, black peppercorns, cloves, cinnamon stick and bay leaf. Let this sizzle so the oil is infused with the first layer of flavour. Next, add the onions and cook gently for at least 15 minutes until they are deep golden brown and caramelized but not burnt. Add the crushed garlic and green chillies, sauté for about a minute, then add the tomato paste, ground spices and fenugreek leaves. Gently cook out for about a minute, then pour in the blitzed plum tomatoes. Stir well, cover and cook for at least 15 minutes over a low heat until you see oil floating to the surface (this means your ground spices have been cooked out).

Gently place the meatballs into the sauce, ideally in one layer. Cover and simmer for 5 minutes, then stir gently, cover again, and simmer for a further 15 minutes until the meatballs are cooked through. Taste for seasoning, garnish with the chopped coriander and serve with wedges of lemon for squeezing over. Remove the whole spices just before serving, if preferred.

layered plates

When I was discouraged from studying Art at university by my parents, food became a creative outlet, allowing me to express myself on plates rather than canvas. My mind approaches a plate of food in the same way I imagine a painting. There are several layers of sketching, shading and detailing – much like my approach to a dish.

In layered plates the focus is on different flavours, colours and textures, on building sharing plates where vegetables feature heavily; the idea is to make several and share the contrasting layers of flavour.

A base of creamy labneh or feta, bouncy noodles or plump beans helps to bind the seasonal bounty being placed on top. A final drizzle of pesto or chutney, and perhaps a flurry of dukkah or za'atar, makes the layered plate sing.

Naturally, in a chapter all about layers, I couldn't resist including a lasagne recipe, and this one celebrates mushrooms, with layers of miso and harissa for a deep umami flavour.

Unpeel every layer to celebrate a dish built with this philosophy in mind.

vietnamese street fries

If there was ever a universal language in food, that dialect is called fries!
Nearly every country in the world has its own version of fries.

The UK has fish and chips, the USA burger and fries, France has moules
frites, and on the streets of Vietnam, I found these street fries. Said to be
inspired by the banh mi, this recipe has no real measurements. Use
the below sauces and shower on the dressings and toppings to your
heart's desire.

This is pure happiness – serve on a big baking tray and let everyone share
from the same platter – food shouldn't be too serious!

Frozen French fries (2 handfuls
  per person)
Sriracha
Kewpie Japanese mayonnaise, but
  any mayo is fine (or use sriracha
  mayonnaise and skip the sriracha)
Sweet hoisin sauce
Sliced spring onions (scallions)
Crushed salted peanuts
Mixed sesame seeds
Chopped coriander (cilantro) or
  coriander cress, to garnish

Cook the fries according to the packet instructions, usually
about 18–20 minutes in the oven.

Start to layer the sauces in a criss-cross fashion. Being a creature
of habit I begin with sriracha, mayonnaise, hoisin and finish with
spring onions, peanuts, sesame seeds and coriander. Be super-
generous and quick – these will be demolished fast!

roasted harissa carrots with whipped feta & crispy chickpeas

I've only become acquainted with harissa in the last five years, but given that it's such an instant flavour bomb, it's my new best friend in a jar for dinner parties. The texture in this dish comes from dukkah, an Egyptian nut, seed and spice blend. You will find it in supermarkets, but it's also very easy to make at home. The recipe below makes extra, so you can store it and use to sprinkle over hummus, soups and salads.

Serves 4

8 carrots (about 500g/1lb 2oz in total)
1½ tsp rose harissa
1 tsp extra virgin olive oil
Wild rocket (arugula), to garnish

For the crispy chickpeas
1 x 400g (14oz) can of chickpeas (or use any other beans), drained and rinsed
½ tsp baharat (or garam masala)
Pinch of sea salt
Squeeze of honey
Drizzle of extra virgin olive oil

For the whipped feta
200g (7oz) good-quality feta
100g (3½oz) thick Greek yogurt
1 lemon, for zesting

For the coriander zhoug
100g (3½oz) coriander (cilantro) stems (leaves and stalks)
1 fresh green jalapeño
2 garlic cloves, peeled
Seeds of 2 cardamom pods, crushed
5 tbsp extra virgin olive oil
Juice of ½ lemon

For the dukkah (or use shop-bought)
70g (2½oz) mixed nuts, such as hazelnuts, cashews, walnuts, almonds
1 tbsp cumin seeds
1 tbsp fennel seeds
1 tbsp coriander seeds
4 tbsp sesame seeds
1 tsp sunflower seeds
Sea salt and ground pepper, to taste

Preheat the oven to 200°C/400°F/gas mark 6.

Scrub your carrots (no need to peel), cut in half lengthways and place in a baking tray. Coat all over in the harissa and olive oil (I use my hands, but wash thoroughly afterwards). Pat the chickpeas dry, transfer to a separate baking tray and coat with the baharat (or garam masala), salt, honey and olive oil. Place both trays in the oven and roast for 30 minutes.

Meanwhile, add the feta and yogurt to a food processor and process until light and airy. This will take 3–5 minutes, so be patient. Once ready, transfer to a large, flat plate and grate over some lemon zest.

Blitz together all the ingredients for the coriander zhoug until it forms a pesto-like texture, then set aside.

If making your own dukkah, toast your nuts of choice in a dry frying pan for about 3 minutes over a medium heat, shaking occasionally. Now add the spices, toast for a further 2 minutes, then transfer to a pestle and mortar and bash the nuts and spices together. Add the sesame and sunflower seeds and season with salt and pepper. Store in a screw-top jar.

Assemble by placing the warm carrots on top of the whipped feta, scatter over the chickpeas, add a drizzle of zhoug and a sprinkling of dukkah. Use a few sprigs of wild rocket to garnish. Best eaten immediately, with fresh bread.

If you want to get ahead, all the elements can be made a few hours in advance; just reheat the carrots and chickpeas.

{pictured right, overleaf}

gochujang lamb chops with summery noodle slaw

Minimum effort for maximum flavour, these lamb chops might be the prettiest I've ever seen. A BBQ recipe I make in the summer, and also on colder days pan-fried or roasted in the oven, as here.

Serves 4

8 lamb cutlet chops
1 tbsp ginger and garlic paste (see page 180 for homemade)
3 tbsp mixed sesame seeds
Finely chopped chives (or the green part of spring onions/scallions)

For the Korean marinade and sauce
2 tbsp gochujang paste
3 tbsp honey
2 tbsp sesame oil
2 tbsp kecap manis (or soy sauce)

For the noodle slaw
300g (10½oz) vermicelli rice noodles
2 carrots, cut into matchsticks
½ cucumber, middle seedy bit removed, cut into matchsticks
10 radishes, finely sliced
Handful of fresh herbs, such as coriander (cilantro) and mint

1 quantity of nuoc cham dressing (page 180)

In a bowl, coat the lamb chops in the ginger and garlic paste. Mix together all the ingredients for the Korean sauce and use half to coat the lamb chops. Cover and leave to marinate for at least 1 hour (in the fridge if longer).

Meanwhile, prepare the noodle slaw. Soak the noodles in just-boiled water for 5 minutes, then drain and rinse. Mix the carrots, cucumber, radishes, herbs and noodles together and set aside.

The lamb chops can now be pan-fried (or roasted, see note below) when your guests arrive as they are super-quick to cook. Bring the lamb chops to room temperature, if necessary, and cook in a frying or griddle pan over a high heat for 3 minutes on each side, basting with the remaining Korean marinade as you go. This will achieve a medium-rare chop. If your chops are quite thick, you may need an extra 3–5 minutes in the oven.

Rest the chops for 5–7 minutes, brush a little more marinade over them and generously sprinkle over the sesame seeds. Garnish with chives or spring onions.

To serve, dress the slaw with the nuoc cham dressing and arrange the salad on a platter, with the lamb chops on top.

Note
To cook the chops in the oven, sear in the pan for 1 minute each side, before roasting in an oven preheated to 200°C/400°F/gas mark 6 for 12 minutes, basting halfway through.

{pictured left, overleaf}

crispy sambal chicken wings
(*ayam penyet*)

It was a magical moment when I tried fried chicken with this addictive sambal on the streets of Seminyak, Bali. I thought I'd never be able to have KFC again without this sambal.

They bashed the chicken legs against a large stone with a pestle. I almost urged them to stop, wondering why they were ruining the crispy fried chicken! Trust the process: the bashing enhances the flavour and allows the fiery sambal to seep into the chicken. This is an addictive combination.

Chicken wings might not be an obvious dinner-party dish, but I love how tender the flesh is and how crispy you can get the skin. It's very forgiving and impossible to overcook! I appreciate not everyone likes to deep-fry at home, so I developed this oven (or air-fryer) version to mimic fried chicken. The sambal is great to have in your armour for a number of dishes, including fish, noodle, curries and meat. These wings are gorgeous with just the sambal, or served as a main with fragrant coconut rice (page 185) and cucumber wedges.

Serves 4

20 skin-on chicken wings (or 8 skin-on, bone-in chicken thighs)
50g (1¾oz) rice flour
25g (1oz) cornflour (cornstarch)
1 tbsp baking powder
1 tsp garlic powder
1 tsp ground turmeric
Generous grind of black pepper
Sea salt, to taste
Spray oil
Thai basil leaves, to garnish

For the sambal
5 large red chillies (or 3 bird's eye)
2 vine tomatoes
2 shallots (or ½ onion)
3 small garlic cloves, peeled
Thumb-sized piece of fresh ginger, peeled
3 fresh makrut lime leaves
½ tsp ground turmeric
½ tsp coriander seeds
1 tsp palm sugar or white sugar
½ tsp sea salt
Juice of 1 lime
1 tbsp extra virgin coconut oil

Preheat the oven to 200°C/400°F/gas mark 6.

Pat your chicken dry with kitchen paper; this will ensure very crispy skin. Place in a roasting tray. Mix the flours, baking powder, spices and salt together, then use to coat the chicken all over. Spray with a little oil and roast in the oven for 45 minutes (or in an air-fryer for 20 minutes).

Meanwhile, put all the ingredients for the sambal except the coconut oil in a blender and blitz until fine. Heat the coconut oil in a pan over a medium heat and stir-fry the sambal in the oil for about 5 minutes.

Once the chicken wings are cooked and crispy, use a rolling pin to gently bash open, then spoon over some of the sambal and garnish with Thai basil leaves.

fig, mozzarella & aleppo cashews

September marks the short fig season in the UK. Pairing with creamy mozzarella and the spicy crunch from the cashews is lazy entertaining at its best; there is no hands-on cooking involved. Platters like this let the canvas of nature impress. Serve with chunky bread and maybe the spicy gochujang rigatoni on page 124, for a main course.

Serves 4

70g (2½oz) wild rocket (arugula)
2 balls of good-quality mozzarella, drained
4 figs, quartered
2 tbsp extra virgin olive oil
1 tbsp pomegranate molasses
Handful of mint leaves
Sea salt and ground pepper, to taste

For the Aleppo cashews
50g (1¾oz) cashews
1 tsp olive oil
1 tbsp Aleppo pepper
½ tsp ground turmeric
Squeeze of honey

Preheat the oven to 180°C/350°F/gas mark 4.

Spread the cashews out in a large baking tray and roast in the oven for 8 minutes.

Meanwhile, in a bowl, mix the olive oil, Aleppo pepper, turmeric, honey and some salt together. Remove the cashews from the oven and mix them in the dressing to coat. Return them to the oven to roast for a further 2 minutes.

Next, arrange the rocket on a large flat platter, tear the mozzarella into irregular pieces and place on top of the rocket, then nestle in the fig quarters.

Sprinkle over the roasted cashews, and drizzle the extra virgin olive oil and pomegranate molasses over the salad. Sprinkle over the mint leaves, season with sea salt and pepper, and serve.

asian hispi cabbage with tahini butter beans, peas & chilli oil

Cabbage is sexy. That sounds so wrong, but cooked like this, hispi is the sexiest 'sweetheart' of the cabbage family. Paired with butter beans, it's unbelievable as a main or as a side. When vegetables are celebrated like this, they have the power to steal the limelight from any joint of juicy meat.

I first had hispi cabbage made like this at a vegan friend's BBQ. I couldn't wait to recreate it, so here is my version – accidentally vegan, and delicious.

Serves 2 as a main, 4 as a side

1 tbsp rapeseed (canola) oil
1 hispi (also known as pointed
   or sweetheart) cabbage (about
   400g/14oz), cut lengthways into
   quarters, core and all
40ml (1½fl oz) water
4 spring onions (scallions), finely
   chopped
3 garlic cloves, finely chopped
3cm (1¼-inch) piece of fresh ginger,
   peeled and grated
2 tbsp light soy sauce
1 tbsp oyster sauce
1 tsp sesame oil

For the tahini butter beans

1 x 600g (1lb 5oz) butter beans
   (lima beans), drained and rinsed
100g (3½oz) frozen peas, thawed
100g (3½oz) edamame beans (optional)
2 tbsp tahini (ensure runny)
Juice of ½ lime
Pinch of sea salt

To garnish

2 tbsp chilli oil (see page 179
   for homemade)
2 tbsp mixed sesame seeds
1 tbsp crushed peanuts (optional)

Mix together all the ingredients for the tahini butter beans and set aside.

Next, rub a little of the oil all over the cabbage wedges. Heat a large non-stick frying pan (that has a lid) over a medium-high heat, then when hot, add the wedges, on a flat side. Leave to cook without moving them for 2–3 minutes until charred, then flip to the other flat side. Once charred, flip onto the rounded side, add the water, cover with a lid and leave to steam for 5 minutes. Remove and set aside on a plate.

To the same pan, add the remaining oil and stir-fry the spring onions, garlic and ginger for about 2 minutes. Add the soy and oyster sauces with a splash of water to loosen, let this bubble for about 1 minute, then return the cabbage to the pan to coat. Take off the heat and drizzle over the sesame oil.

To assemble, spoon the tahini butter beans and peas onto a large platter, arrange the cabbage wedges on top, drizzle over some chilli oil, and sprinkle over the sesame seeds and crushed peanuts (if using).

blood orange & za'atar burrata with hazelnuts

Pairing fruit and cheese together is nothing new. Cheddar and pineapple is a British dinner-party staple from the 1980s, and I firmly believe all these 'trendy' cheese and fruit combinations have been inspired by this retro classic! In season, from February to April, blood oranges are just divine, and persimmons are wonderful from October to December. Be creative and use peaches, pears or grapefruit too, but please let the seasons guide you.

Serves 4

3 oranges
2 large burrata
30g (1oz) toasted hazelnuts,
   roughly chopped
Handful of basil and mint leaves

For the dressing
2 tbsp extra virgin olive oil
½ garlic clove, crushed
1 tbsp za'atar
1 tsp Aleppo pepper
1 tbsp capers
Squeeze of lemon juice
Squeeze of honey

First make the dressing by mixing everything together in a screw-top jar. This will keep in the fridge for up to 3 days.

Top and tail the oranges, then following their natural curve, cut away the skin and any pith, using a small, sharp serrated knife. Cut into rounds, about 1cm (½ inch) thick.

Place the burrata in the middle of a large platter and arrange the orange slices around it. Drizzle over the dressing and sprinkle over the hazelnuts, and the basil and mint leaves.

crispy herb & chilli silken tofu

Silken tofu is a very curious cousin of the firm spongy tofu you might be used to; it's a creamy, wobbly tofu that reminds me of panna cotta. Here I am topping it with crunchy bits and umami flavour bombs. You can buy fresh or long-life silken tofu (which can be stored in your cupboard) so it's a great last-minute champion for entertaining. This is a beautiful starter, especially on a hot summer's day. It's equally wonderful on top of sticky rice, for a bigger sharing feast.

Silken tofu can also be whipped in a food processor and used as a vegan alternative to yogurt or cheese in other recipes.

Serves 4

2 x 340g (12oz) packs of silken tofu
   (bean curd)
200ml (7fl oz) vegetable oil
15g (½oz) each of coriander (cilantro)
   and Thai basil, leaves only
5 spring onions (scallions), finely sliced
5 garlic cloves, sliced

For the dressing
1 tbsp Korean gochugaru chilli flakes
   (or regular chilli flakes)
1 tbsp sugar
2 tbsp light soy sauce
2 tbsp Chinkiang black vinegar
   (or rice vinegar)
1 tbsp sesame oil
1 tbsp white sesame seeds

In a bowl, mix together all the ingredients for the dressing.

Tip the silken tofu upside down onto a nice plate or into a shallow bowl. Score it very gently so the dressing will seep into the grooves. Pour the dressing over the tofu.

Put the oil in a deep frying pan and place over a medium heat until it reads 180°C (356°F) on a cooking thermometer, or a small piece of bread dropped into the oil sizzles and turns golden brown in 5–7 seconds.

Use tongs to carefully lower the coriander and Thai basil leaves, in batches, into the hot oil. Deep-fry for about 1 minute, then remove to kitchen paper to drain. Repeat with the spring onions and garlic, until the garlic turns golden. When the tofu is cool enough to handle, garnish with the crispy aromatics.

roast beetroot with whipped goat's cheese & thai pesto

Some dishes are too pretty to eat. Well, beetroot makes everything pretty; whichever way you try to plate this up, it will look beautiful. This is the first dish Peter Jones, of Dragons' Den, tried when I cooked for him, and he said if this is just the start then I can't wait for what's to come because you've just set the bar super-high!

Beetroot with goat's cheese is a classic combination that works, and by adding a Thai-inspired pesto and some crunch from the pistachios, it's been elevated and made more interesting. Be really cheffy and buy some beetroot dust to really impress! Many elements can be made in advance, so you only need to assemble when your guests arrive. This is a great starter or a sharing salad with other small plates.

Serves 4

6 raw beetroots (beets), or use ready-to-eat (with no vinegar) and skip the roasting step
100g (3½oz) goat's cheese
200g (7oz) coconut yogurt (or Greek yogurt)
Zest of 1 lime
Pinch of sea salt
Thai pesto (see page 182), to serve

To garnish
Handful of crushed pistachios
Coriander (cilantro) cress (or a few Thai basil leaves)
Beetroot (beet) dust, for dusting

Preheat the oven to 200°C/400°F/gas mark 6.

Top and tail the beetroots, wash and prick with a fork before wrapping in foil and roasting for 1 hour.

Put the goat's cheese and yogurt with the lime zest and salt into a clean food processor and blitz until light and airy. Either store in the fridge for later or start to assemble and spoon onto a wide sharing platter or on individual plates.

Poke a knife through the middle of a beetroot to ensure it is fully cooked, then remove them to a board and cut into wedges. Arrange over the whipped goat's cheese, spoon on the pesto in a random fashion and sprinkle over the crushed pistachios. Delicately arrange coriander cress or a few small Thai basil leaves over the top. Dust with beetroot powder on one half of the dish and plate. Marvel over the pretty dish you've just made and serve it proudly to your guests.

tajín watermelon & halloumi

There is nothing new about pairing watermelon and feta. However, upgrade this to warm halloumi with a sprinkling of tajín – a Mexican chilli seasoning – and this summery salad has margarita vibes! Absolutely everyone asks me for this recipe, but there is no big secret – just buy yourself a bottle of tajín online or at a specialist food store.

Again, so simple to put together. It's also wonderful on the BBQ (grill) or just done on a griddle pan, as here. Serve on its own with some fresh crusty bread as a starter, or with some grilled chicken such as my peri peri thighs on page 75.

Serves 4

1 mini watermelon (or 600g /1lb 5oz), rind removed, cut into slices
2 x 250g (9oz) packs of halloumi, cut into 1.5cm (¾-inch) slices
1 red onion, finely sliced
Handful of coriander (cilantro), basil and mint leaves, or rocket (arugula)
Lime wedges, to serve

For the dressing
5 tbsp extra virgin olive oil
1 tbsp tajín seasoning (or Aleppo pepper)
Juice of 1 lime
1 garlic clove, crushed

Arrange the watermelon slices on a large platter.

Mix together all the ingredients for the dressing and set aside.

Heat a non-stick frying pan or griddle over a medium heat, add your halloumi and cook (without any oil) for about 2 minutes until golden brown, then reduce the heat and cook the other side for a further minute, until golden brown. Transfer to the plate with the watermelon, scatter over the red onion and herbs, then drizzle over the dressing. Serve with lime wedges.

thai pomelo salad
(*yum som o*)

While cycling around Chiang Mai, northern Thailand, on our honeymoon, we stopped at a cart with a petite lady bashing together chillies with a pyramid of these huge citrus fruits the size of small watermelons around her. I had never seen a pomelo before. Like a curious kid, I watched her tear away the thick skin to reveal a grapefruit-like pink interior but every segment was larger, not as juicy, milder, sweeter and less acidic than grapefruit. It was an unforgettable and memorable moment. Pomelo is the largest member of the citrus family, the ancestor of the grapefruit and native to Southeast Asia.

For me, the Thai pomelo salad epitomizes that union of hot, sour, salty and sweet, which is the backbone of the Thai flavour balance. Yum som o is not as fiery-hot as its green papaya cousin som tam, and this is why I prefer it. Try to seek out pomelo, available in Asian stores. Otherwise, grapefruit is a good substitute.

This would make a wonderful starter to any of my Asian curries, or served as a side. As always, the focus is to keep things simple and not feel overwhelmed. Lots of make-ahead elements below – it's more of an assembly dish.

Serves 4

1 pomelo (or 2 grapefruit)
2 shallots, finely sliced
2 lemongrass stalks, white part only, finely sliced
2 fresh makrut lime leaves, central stems removed, finely sliced
2 tbsp crushed salted peanuts
4 tbsp toasted shredded coconut (or use coarse desiccated/shredded)
Small equal handfuls of coriander (cilantro), mint and Thai basil, leaves only
1 red chilli, to garnish (optional)

For the dressing
2 red bird's eye chillies
1 tbsp palm sugar or caster (superfine) sugar
1 tbsp fish sauce
Juice of 2 limes

Start by prepping your pomelo (or grapefruit). Cut in half from top to bottom, remove the thick outer peel, then remove the membrane from around each segment. Arrange the segments over a large platter. Keep in the fridge in a covered container if not using immediately; it will keep really well.

Make the dressing by bashing the chillies in a pestle and mortar, until pulpy. Add the sugar, fish sauce and lime juice, and mix together. Set aside, or store in a screw-top jar in the fridge if using later.

To assemble, over the pomelo layer the shallots, lemongrass, lime leaves, peanuts, toasted coconut and all the herbs. Spoon over the dressing and add a final garnish of red chilli for its pop of colour, if you like.

harissa salmon with rocket chimichurri & za'atar roast potatoes

Accidental recipes from fridge raids seem to be my best inventions; pairing together ingredients to use up before they get thrown out gives me such a buzz! After an indulgent Christmas I still had copious amounts of potatoes and wild rocket to use up. Here is the result: sunset-red salmon against a bright green chimichurri with rocket leaves destined for the bin! It's a great dinner party dish where everyone helps themselves to a truly restaurant-worthy meal.

Serves 4

4 salmon fillets, each about 120g (4oz)
2 tbsp rose harissa
1 tsp runny honey
Sea salt and ground pepper, to taste

For the za'atar garlic potatoes
1kg (2lb 3oz) baby new potatoes
25g (1oz) butter, cut into cubes
3 garlic cloves, crushed
1 tbsp za'atar
2 tbsp olive oil
Small bunch of parsley, chopped
    (optional)

To serve
Rocket chimichurri (see page 183)
Green salad or steamed greens

Place the salmon fillets in a baking tray and rub the harissa all over them. Drizzle over the honey, sprinkle with a tiny bit of salt and set aside.

Preheat the oven to 190°C/375°F/gas mark 5.

Meanwhile scrub (don't peel) your potatoes, cut in half and cook in boiling water for about 8 minutes. Drain and transfer to a second baking tray. Add the cubes of butter, garlic, za'atar, olive oil, and salt and pepper to taste. Roast in the oven for 25 minutes, shaking once halfway through.

Add the salmon baking tray to the oven and cook alongside the potatoes for 15 minutes.

Remove the potatoes and salmon from the oven and sprinkle the parsley, if using, over the potatoes. Serve the salmon on top of the potatoes, with the chimichurri in a bowl on the table for everyone to help themselves, and a green salad or some steamed greens.

miso mushroom
& lentil lasagne

My mum is a vegetarian who doesn't like to eat anything that mimics meat
and doesn't eat eggs, despite not being vegan. This lasagne is the closest
I've got to a meaty lasagne with no soya products, and thankfully my mum
loves it. At Christmas this is often the main course she will ask for and
enjoy with the bounty of roast potatoes – who says carb on carb shouldn't
be allowed?

Serves 4

500g (1lb 2oz) chestnut mushrooms
50ml (2fl oz) olive oil
2 onions, finely diced
2 carrots, finely diced
6 garlic cloves, crushed
1 heaped tbsp rose harissa
2 tbsp tomato purée (paste)
1 vegetable stock cube
300ml (10fl oz) boiling water
1 tbsp miso paste
1 pouch (250g/9oz) of ready-cooked
    Puy lentils (or canned lentilles vertes)
25g (1oz) each of basil and parsley
    leaves, chopped
30ml (2 tbsp) double (heavy) cream
100g (3½oz) Parmesan, grated
250g (9oz) dried lasagne sheets
100g (3½oz) Cheddar, grated
Sea salt and ground pepper, to taste
Rocket (arugula) salad, to serve

Preheat the oven to 200°C/400°F/gas mark 6.

In a food processor, blitz the mushrooms in batches until finely
diced. Place on a flat baking tray, drizzle over half the olive oil
and roast for 40 minutes, mixing them halfway. Turn the oven
down to 190°C/375°F/gas mark 5.

Meanwhile, in a pan, sauté the onions and carrots in the
remaining olive oil until soft but not coloured. Add the garlic,
stir for a minute, then add the harissa, tomato purée and the
roasted mushrooms. Dissolve the stock cube in the boiling
water, with the miso paste stirred through. Add the liquid to the
mushroom pan and tip in the lentils. Let the mixture simmer
for at least 10 minutes, then take off the heat and add the herbs.
Drizzle in half the cream, to give the mixture a velvety finish; it
should be pourable but not soup-like. Taste for seasoning and get
ready to assemble.

Grab a baking tray or dish, about 25 x 30cm (10 x 12 inches).
Start with a layer of the mushroom and lentil mixture, sprinkle
over some Parmesan and cover with a layer of lasagne sheets.
Continue in this fashion until you reach the top, finishing with
a pasta layer. Cover in the remaining cream, the Cheddar and a
final sprinkling of Parmesan.

Bake in the oven for 45 minutes, until bubbling and the lasagne
is cooked, then remove and leave to stand for 10 minutes before
cutting. Serve with a rocket salad.

beetroot, avocado & artichoke salad

This is my default salad. So impressive and easy to put together, with vacuum-packed, ready-to-eat beetroot that lasts ages in the fridge, and a jar of artichokes. Using shortcuts wherever you can is your dinner-party trick for effortless entertaining. A perfect salad for a BBQ, or to accompany pasta or risotto.

Serves 4

90g (3¼oz) mixed leaves with rocket (arugula)
2 ready-to-eat cooked beetroot (beets), sliced
1 x 250g (9oz) jar of artichokes
1 large avocado, halved, pitted, peeled and sliced into half-moons
1 red onion, thinly sliced
10 baby plum tomatoes, halved
30g (1oz) mixed seeds
4 tbsp extra virgin olive oil
2 tbsp balsamic vinegar

Arrange the mixed leaves on a platter. Layer over all the vegetables, sprinkle over the seeds and drizzle over the olive oil and balsamic vinegar.

{pictured right, overleaf}

grilled lemon courgettes with cardamom labneh

I've recently developed a fascination with layering vegetables over something creamy and adding some crunchy bits, commonly referred to as the Ottolenghi effect. It's a beautiful way to highlight the flavours of vegetables. The combination in the labneh of cardamom and curry leaf oil gives off an Indian vibe, while the lemony courgettes bring to mind the antipasti from the Amalfi coast. This dish has no boundaries or rules, allowing for culinary magic to happen. It is perfect for entertaining and can be prepared ahead of time, served as a starter or a side dish to chicken, or as part of your mezze spread.

Serves 4

4 pitta breads (shop-bought), cut
    into squares
1 tbsp extra virgin olive oil
1 tbsp za'atar
2 tbsp vegetable oil
20 fresh curry leaves
1 tsp Aleppo pepper (or regular chilli
    flakes with a pinch of paprika)
Handful of coriander (cilantro) leaves

For the labneh*
4 green cardamom pods, seeds crushed
½ tsp sea salt
500g (1lb 2oz) Greek yogurt

For the grilled courgettes
3 large courgettes (zucchini), sliced
    lengthways about 3mm (⅛in) thick
2 garlic cloves, crushed
Juice of 1 lemon
1 tbsp extra virgin olive oil
Sea salt, to taste

*Note: Labneh is simply strained
    yogurt, with the profile of thick,
    soft cheese. It's extremely easy to
    make but does take 24 hours to
    strain, so if you are short of time,
    simply buy extra thick Greek
    yogurt, or mix half yogurt with
    half cream cheese.

If you are making the labneh, start 24 hours beforehand. Otherwise, use extra thick yogurt (10% fat). Mix the crushed cardamom seeds and salt into the yogurt and stir well. Place a fine sieve (strainer) over a large bowl. Line it with a piece of muslin (cheesecloth) and spoon in the yogurt mixture. Knot the top of the cloth to make a snug bundle. Place something heavy on top and leave to drain in the fridge for 24 hours.

The next day, put the courgettes, garlic, lemon juice, olive oil and salt in a large bowl and leave to marinate for 30 minutes (if you would like to get ahead, you can prep this step and leave in the fridge with the labneh).

Take the labneh out of the fridge, unwrap the cloth, and spread it out on a platter, ready for the courgettes to be draped over.

Coat the pitta squares in the olive oil and za'atar. Heat a frying pan over a medium heat, add the pitta and stir-fry for a few minutes until crispy, then remove from the pan and set aside.

Heat a griddle pan until hot. In batches, place the courgette slices on the griddle pan and cook for 2–3 minutes on each side, then place on top of the labneh.

Heat the vegetable oil in a small pan, add the curry leaves and let them sizzle and infuse the oil, then remove from the heat.

Scatter the pitta croutons over the courgettes, then finish the plate with a sprinkle of Aleppo pepper and the curry leaves.

{pictured left, overleaf}

last minute guests

The best relationship you can have is with your store cupboard. Here I rely mainly on pantry ingredients to whip up tasty meals in minutes for last-minute guests.

I think I have subconsciously adopted this approach from my mum, who would have endless stocks of dried lentils, beans, dehydrated rice flakes and tins of everything imaginable in her pantry.

My cupboards overflow with pasta, noodles, rice and jars of sticky condiments. The freezer has a selection of dumplings, curry pastes, crushed ginger/garlic and breads. The dry store and freezer are always sources of inspiration when I haven't done a grocery shop or when friends drop in.

My mum would never let anyone leave the house without eating something; in our busy lives, where this isn't always possible, a coffee and some cookies are always happily received. However, if you do need some quick inspiration for something more substantial, this section ticks that box – not only for last-minute guests but also last-minute after-work saviours.

gochujang rigatoni

Since I've made you buy a tub of gochujang, let's make use of it! A reliable store-cupboard staple, this is a wonderful way to use this sticky chilli paste in a pasta dish. It delivers all the flavour with minimum effort. Inspired by pasta alla vodka, this Asian version takes it up a notch! Serve with one of my salads for a beautiful easy dinner-party menu, or on its own for last-minute drop-ins! Feel free to add chicken, prawns (shrimp) or sausages to this recipe.

Serves 4

400g (14oz) dried rigatoni pasta
1 tbsp unsalted butter
1 tbsp olive oil
1 shallot, finely chopped
5 garlic cloves, crushed
2 tbsp gochujang paste
150ml (5fl oz) double (heavy) cream
Sea salt, to taste
Freshly ground black pepper (optional)

To serve (optional)
Chopped chives
Grated Parmesan
Extra virgin olive oil

Cook the pasta in a big pot of heavily salted, boiling water, for about 8 minutes or until al dente.

Meanwhile, melt the butter with the olive oil in a pan over a low–medium heat. Add the shallot and garlic and lightly sauté for 30 seconds until fragrant.

Add the gochujang and cook down for about a minute to release the paste's flavours. Next, add the cream and gently stir until the gochujang is evenly distributed throughout and the cream becomes a rosy pink colour.

Drain the pasta and reserve half a cup of the pasta cooking water. Add the drained pasta to the sauce, with a ladleful of the reserved pasta water, and mix until evenly coated, adding more water if needed. Simmer over a low heat for 2 minutes, then remove from the heat and serve immediately, with a sprinkling of chives, a generous grating of Parmesan, and a drizzle of extra virgin olive oil if you like, and an optional twist of black pepper.

cheat's turkish manti

Manti is a traditional Turkish dish of meat-filled dumplings, usually lamb, with the same beautiful marriage of ingredients as the Turkish eggs on page 68. Use frozen dumplings or shop-bought fresh tortelloni to make this winning dish to wow your guests. I hold no snobbery for a good shortcut; in fact – I live for it – it's like getting a bargain in the sales when you were about to buy it at full price! Enjoy this natural high!

Serves 2

20 frozen chicken, veg or meat gyoza
OR
300g (10½oz) shop-bought fresh filled
  tortelloni (any of your choice)
Sprinkling of dried mint or finely
  chopped fresh mint

For the yogurt sauce
1 garlic clove, crushed to a paste
300g (10½oz) Greek yogurt
Sea salt, to taste

For the chilli butter
25g (1oz) salted butter
1 tbsp Aleppo pepper (or regular chilli
  flakes with a pinch of paprika)
2 tbsp pine nuts (optional)

Mix the garlic into the yogurt, add salt to taste, mix and set aside. This can be gently heated if preferred, or brought to room temperature, but I like the contrast of cold, creamy yogurt against the hot dumplings.

Now melt the butter in a pan until foaming and turning slightly brown, then add the Aleppo pepper and pine nuts (if using), swirl it around, let it foam and combine for a minute, then take off the heat.

Steam the gyoza or boil the tortelloni according to the packet instructions.

Grab a large platter, spread the yogurt over the base, place the dumplings or tortelloni on top, pour over the chilli butter and sprinkle over the mint. Share and enjoy, or create individual plates of this delicious concoction.

creamiest hummus ever

Homemade hummus is a beautiful thing. Keep a jar of tahini and a can of chickpeas in your pantry, and this gesture will bring joy to your guests who have just dropped in, served with pitta chips. Literally takes 5 minutes!

Makes about 500g (1lb 2oz)

400g (14oz) drained chickpeas (from a
    can or jar; save the liquid)
2 garlic cloves, peeled
3 tbsp tahini
1 tbsp olive oil
Juice of 1 lemon
5 ice cubes
50ml (2fl oz) reserved chickpea liquid
Sea salt, to taste

To finish
Ground cumin
Sumac
Olive oil
Harissa butter (if feeling fancy;
    see method)

Blitz all the ingredients for the hummus in a blender, adding the chickpea liquid gradually. Keep blending until you have a smooth, velvety texture.

Swirl onto a plate, sprinkle over some ground cumin, sumac and olive oil. If you are feeling fancy, melt some butter in a small pan until foaming, take off heat and stir in ½ teaspoon of rose harissa to drizzle over.

{pictured left}

sizzling chilli yogurt

Anything to share and dunk over drinks with friends is perfection.
If you have some Greek yogurt and a couple of spring onions, make this chilli yogurt and dunk pitta bread or even scoop up with tortilla crisps or prawn crackers.

Serves 4

400g (14oz) thick Greek yogurt
3 spring onions (scallions), finely
    chopped
2 garlic cloves, crushed
3 tsp Korean gochugaru chilli flakes (or
    regular chilli flakes)
1 tsp sesame seeds
Handful of chopped coriander (cilantro)
70ml (2¼fl oz) olive oil
Sea salt, to taste

Swirl the yogurt onto a large plate and sprinkle with salt.

Put the spring onions, garlic, chilli flakes, sesame seeds and coriander in a heatproof bowl, with a pinch of salt.

Heat the oil in a small pan over a high heat for 2–3 minutes, then carefully pour into the bowl; it will sizzle and quickly cook the aromatics. Let stand for a couple of minutes to infuse.

Pour the contents of the bowl over the yogurt and serve.

10-minute nasi goreng

This is your signal to use up leftover rice. Never attempt to make nasi goreng with fresh rice. Its history lies in preventing food waste in Indonesia, an idea also prevalent in many other regions of the world. It makes me so happy to see rice in the fridge ready to be recycled! Warning: don't keep cooked rice for longer than 24 hours – ready-cooked packet rice is brilliant for this.

Serves 2

2 tbsp rapeseed (canola) oil, plus extra
   for the eggs
2 garlic cloves, crushed
1 red chilli, chopped
3 spring onions (scallions), chopped
Finely chopped vegetables of your
   choice, such as (bell) peppers, green
   beans, baby corn, carrots
100g (3½oz) leftover roast chicken
   (optional)
500g (1lb 2oz) leftover white rice (or
   ready-cooked packet rice)
2 tbsp kecap manis, plus extra to finish
1 tsp light soy sauce
2 eggs
Ground white pepper, to taste

To finish
Sliced cucumber and tomatoes
Chilli oil (see page 179 for homemade)
Sesame seeds
Crispy shallots (shop-bought)

Heat the oil in a frying pan or wok over a high heat, add the garlic, chilli and spring onions and stir-fry for a few minutes. Add your chosen vegetables and the cooked chicken (if using) and stir-fry for about 4–5 minutes. Add the cooked rice, kecap manis, soy sauce and some white pepper. Stir-fry until fully coated, then remove from the heat and set aside.

Fry the eggs in a separate pan to your liking; I prefer the yolks runny. Place the fried rice in a bowl and turn upside down onto a plate to achieve a dome. Place a fried egg on top.

Arrange the cucumber and tomatoes on the side. Drizzle some chilli oil and kecap manis on the egg, and sprinkle all over with sesame seeds and crispy shallots.

{pictured right, overleaf}

10-minute tantanmen ramen

A creamy bowl of plant-based ramen made in 10 minutes without the hours of simmering, but with all the flavour. Slurp, chat and laugh with this comforting soul bowl.

Serves 2

2 tbsp crispy chilli oil, plus extra
   to garnish
2 tbsp light soy sauce
2 tsp white miso paste
2 tbsp tahini
2 nests of ramen noodles (or instant
   packet noodles without seasoning)
Selection of green veg, such as
   tenderstem broccoli, pak choi (bok
   choy) or green beans
1 vegetable stock cube, dissolved in
   800ml (27fl oz) water
100ml (3½fl oz) soya milk
30g (2oz) toasted sesame seeds
Chilli oil and chopped spring onions
   (scallions), to garnish

Divide the crispy chilli oil, soy sauce, miso and tahini between two large, deep bowls. Set aside.

Cook the noodles and your green veg of choice in the stock for 2–3 minutes, until al dente (they will continue to cook in the broth so you don't want to overcook them). Drain, returning the cooking water to the pan. Add the soya milk and heat for 1 minute.

Divide the soup equally between the bowls, mix well, add the noodles and greens and garnish with the sesame seeds, chilli oil and spring onions.

{pictured left, overleaf}

rice flakes with potato & curry leaves (*poha bateta*)

I urge you to seek out this store-cupboard staple poha, or rice flakes, an iconic Indian breakfast or snack. My mum would always have this on standby for a weekend brunch, especially for unexpected guests. Brunch has become so trendy recently that I thought a dish Indians eat for breakfast or brunch would be really appropriate in this book.

If you haven't come across it before, let me introduce you to poha bateta. Poha (pronounced pa-wa) consists of dehydrated flattened rice flakes, tempered with curry leaves, mustard seeds, ginger, potatoes and lots of lemon – a flavour explosion full of different textures. I also add sweetcorn and peanuts for a crunch and flavour element. Bateta, unsurprisingly, means potato.

Yes, Indians do carb on carb brilliantly! Each Indian household will have its own version and also name it differently. So whether it's bateta powa, pava aloo or poha batata, you really need to give this much-loved Indian dish a try.

Serves 2–3

250g (9oz) medium poha flakes
  (available from Asian stores)
2 tbsp rapeseed (canola) or sunflower oil
1 tsp mustard seeds
1 tsp cumin seeds
15 fresh curry leaves
¼ tsp asafoetida (optional)
1 red onion, finely diced
1 tsp grated fresh ginger
1 green finger chilli, or to taste, chopped
10 par-boiled baby potatoes, halved
Pinch of sugar, to taste (if not adding
  sweetcorn)
100g (3½oz) drained canned sweetcorn
1 tsp ground turmeric
Sea salt, to taste

For the garnish
Plain yogurt
Small handful of roasted peanuts
  or cashews
Coriander (cilantro) leaves
Sprinkle of sev
Lemon wedges

First rinse your poha flakes in a sieve (strainer). Let them stand for about 15 minutes to hydrate. Do not soak them, as the residual moisture from rinsing will be enough to hydrate them.

Heat the oil in a wide pan over a mediu, heat, then add the mustard and cumin seeds and fry until they crackle. Add the curry leaves, asafoetida (if using), onion, ginger and chilli, and stir over a gentle heat for about 3–4 minutes until the onion is translucent.

Add the potatoes and cook to let them absorb the flavours, then add salt to taste (and some sugar if not adding sweetcorn). Once the potatoes are soft, add the sweetcorn and turmeric and stir well.

Tumble in the poha and stir over a low heat until all the flakes are coated and sunshine yellow.

Plate up in bowls and let everyone top their own with yogurt, roasted nuts, coriander, sev and a wedge of lemon for squeezing. Enjoy.

truffle, honey & miso camembert

This is more of a reminder than a recipe. Sometimes you have people dropping in spontaneously, and I love those moments. When I don't want to serve crisps I try to keep a Camembert in my fridge for these eventualities – but if it doesn't happen, it's the perfect weekend treat! An oozing warm Camembert straight out of the oven served with crusty bread is always a crowd pleaser, and with no washing up as it's baked in the box!

Serves 4

2 whole Camembert cheeses
1 small garlic clove, cut into slivers
2 tbsp honey
1 tbsp truffle-infused olive oil
1 tsp miso

To garnish (optional)
Sprigs of thyme
Chilli flakes

To serve
Water biscuits (crackers) or warm
    crusty bread
Optional extras: nuts, such as walnuts
    or almonds for texture, sliced pears,
    grapes, dried apricots or celery sticks

Preheat the oven to 180°C/350°F/gas mark 4.

Remove the wax paper around the cheeses and return the Camemberts to their boxes. Score the rind in a criss-cross diamond fashion and poke the garlic slivers into the gaps.

Mix the honey, truffle-infused oil and miso together and spread it over the cheeses, topping with a few sprigs of thyme and some chilli flakes, if you like.

Bake in the box for 12–15 minutes maximum. Serve immediately with crackers or bread and extras, such as nuts and grapes.

kimchi cheese naan toasties

Use shop-bought naan for an impressive yet humble snack based on the famous cheese toastie, made sexier with trendy kimchi! Mango chutney works equally well. Cut up into cute squares or triangles for a perfect beer snack.

Serves 4

2 large shop-bought garlic and
    coriander naan (or use plain)
150g (5¼oz) mature Cheddar, grated
50g (1¾oz) kimchi or mango chutney

Cover half of each naan with grated cheese, top with kimchi (or mango chutney), fold over and pan-fry on each side for a few minutes until the cheese has melted. Cut into bite-sized pieces.

three-ingredient daal

Giving someone a bowl of daal is like a hug! This is so simple I feel embarrassed calling it a recipe. You simply boil some lentils, use some clever toppings like chilli oil and any other bits you have in the fridge, like broccoli or halloumi. Raid your canned foods and top with chickpeas, or simply serve with bread. Think of this as a soup which needs no blitzing because the lentils are naturally creamy.

Serves 2–3

250g (9oz) red lentils, thoroughly rinsed
450ml (15fl oz) water
2 tsp ground turmeric
20g (¾oz) shop-bought garlic butter
 (or ghee)
Sea salt

Topping ideas
Chilli oil (see page 179 for homemade)
Roasted chickpeas
Griddled halloumi
Roast chicken
Roast aubergine (eggplant)
Steamed broccoli
Crispy tofu
Pitta croutons
Pink onions (see Note)

Put the lentils in a pan, add the water and turmeric and bring to the boil, removing any frothy scum that rises to the surface. Cover and simmer over a medium heat for 20 minutes until creamy. Add the garlic butter (or ghee) at the end, with salt to taste (about a teaspoon).

Serve with any of your chosen toppings.

Note
To make pink onions, finely slice 1 large red onion and place in a screw-top jar. Add the juice of 2 limes and some salt, put the lid on, shake and refrigerate for up to 1 week.

10-minute sticky chinese chicken

Chinese five spice makes for a delicious chicken that can be enjoyed on its own, or with rice noodles, microwave-rice or in a burger bun. The chicken can be griddled on the stove or baked in an air fryer. Rice noodles need only soaking. Microwave-rice needs only 2 minutes. A bun needs only filling. A few clever hacks to put together something delicious for week nights and last-minute friends!

Serves 4

1 tbsp Chinese five spice
1 tsp garlic powder
1 tsp light soy sauce
1 tsp dark soy sauce
2 tbsp olive oil
8 boneless, skinless chicken thighs

To finish
Runny honey, to drizzle
1 red chilli, finely diced
Handful of sesame seeds
1 lime, for squeezing
Handful of chopped coriander (cilantro)

Massage the five spice, garlic powder, soy sauces and olive oil into the chicken thighs, and let rest for 5 minutes (while you chop the chilli and coriander).

Heat a griddle pan until hot, add the chicken and cook for at least 3–4 minutes on each side, pressing down using a spatula to achieve griddle markings (you may need to lower the heat to avoid burning). You can also cook it in an air-fryer at 190°C/375°F for 15 minutes, turning the chicken once halfway.

Check the chicken is cooked through, then remove from the heat and let it rest for 5 minutes. Transfer to a board and cut it into strips. Drizzle over some honey and sprinkle with the chilli, sesame seeds, lime juice and coriander leaves.

Serve as it is, or as suggested above.

sweet plates

This is the hardest chapter for me to write, because growing up desserts were not a big thing. The oven was for storage, not baking! In India most homes did not have an oven and desserts are usually made on the stove, so my mum didn't know how to bake.

Controversially, I am not a fan of Indian desserts. I always found them sickly sweet and lacking texture, and the flavour of cardamom and saffron that perfumed most sweet treats I found overbearing. I think that's why I never took any interest in learning to cook desserts. Pudding protocol would normally involve defrosting a Sara Lee chocolate gateau or slicing a generous wedge of Viennetta ice cream.

If we were feeling really fancy, Mum would get a fruit cocktail out of a can and serve it with custard made out of powder. These were all beautiful nostalgic puddings, but I think my main inspiration came from school dinners. Chocolate sponge with chocolate custard and butterscotch Angel Delight still delight!

I'll show you how to make easy desserts using lots of shortcuts like puff pastry, ready-to-use custard and ginger nut biscuits. There is no judgement here.

This chapter combines exotic flavours I love from travel, eating out and influences absorbed from everywhere – including the ever-changing seasons and landscapes of the British weather!

banoffee pie dumplings

A British dessert with an Asian makeover, this was born in the 2020 lockdown when I was bored of banana bread and had some leftover gyoza skins. A traditional banoffee pie sits on a biscuit base, but these crispy dumplings replace that element. With a coconut caramel instead of toffee sauce, this dessert can be totally plant-based by using vegan cream (or shop-bought vanilla ice cream instead of the chantilly) and vegan chocolate. It's absolutely beautiful and a memorable way to finish your dinner party. All elements can be made ahead of time, with the dumplings fried to serve, as they are best warm.

Serves 4

3 medium bananas, peeled and diced
1 tsp ground cinnamon
1 tsp vanilla bean paste
45g (1½oz) dark muscovado sugar
2 tbsp coconut rum (optional)
16 gyoza wrappers (see page 178 for homemade)
200ml (7fl oz) coconut oil (or rapeseed/canola oil)

For the coconut caramel
1 x 400g (14oz) can of full-fat coconut milk (ideally at least 70% coconut extract)
3 tbsp dark muscovado sugar
Pinch of flaky sea salt

For the vanilla chantilly
250ml (8fl oz) double (heavy) cream
1 tbsp caster (superfine) sugar
½ tsp vanilla bean paste

To serve
Dark chocolate shavings
Chopped pecans (optional)

In a pan, combine the bananas, cinnamon, vanilla, sugar and rum (if using). Place over a low heat and cook for 4–5 minutes until the sugar has melted and the mixture is glossy, then remove from the heat and set aside to cool.

Meanwhile, make the coconut caramel by gently simmering the coconut milk, sugar and salt in a pan over a medium-high heat for about 12 minutes, until it turns into a dark brown, slightly thickened caramel. Remove and set aside.

At this point you can start to assemble the dumplings. Place a tablespoon of the cooled banana mixture in the centre of a gyoza wrapper. Dip your finger in a small bowl of water and run it around the edge of the gyoza wrapper. Fold it over into a half-moon shape and seal, and repeat with the remaining banana mixture and wrappers. The dumplings can at this point be refrigerated for up to 5 hours.

When ready to serve, whisk the ingredients for the vanilla chantilly together until thick, but don't over-whisk or the cream will turn to butter!

Heat the oil in a deep frying pan over a medium heat. When hot, add the dumplings in batches of 4, and fry for 1–2 minutes on each side, until golden. Remove and drain on kitchen paper. Meanwhile, warm the caramel through gently to reheat.

Spoon some caramel into the base of shallow serving bowls, place 4 dumplings per person on top, then add some vanilla chantilly. Grate some chocolate over the top and sprinkle over chopped pecans (if using) to finish.

coconut lime leaf panna cotta with passionfruit & sesame honeycomb

A panna cotta is the best dinner-party dessert that can be made ahead of time. It keeps well in the fridge for up to 3 days and that wobble is just irresistible. More sophisticated than jelly, yet more fun than a posset, a panna cotta has everything going on. Infusing the coconut milk here with lime leaves gives the dessert Thai vibes, which pairs beautifully with any tropical fruits such as pineapple, mango, papaya and lychee. I adore the crunch from the sesame honeycomb that adds an extra texture.

Serves 6

3 large, ripe passionfruit, halved
Thai basil cress or leaves, to decorate
   (optional)

For the panna cotta
3 gelatine leaves
300ml (10fl oz/1¼ cups) double
   (heavy) cream
300ml (10fl oz/1¼ cups) coconut milk
150ml (5fl oz) whole milk
3 fresh makrut lime leaves (optional
   but amazing!)
150g (5¼oz) caster (superfine) sugar

For the sesame honeycomb
100g (3½oz) caster (superfine) sugar
2 tbsp golden syrup
1 tsp bicarbonate of soda (baking soda)
1 tbsp mixed sesame seeds

First soak your gelatine leaves in cold water to hydrate them.

Gently heat the cream, coconut milk, milk and lime leaves (if using) in a saucepan over a medium heat. When it starts to simmer, add the sugar, stirring to dissolve, then bring to the boil and quickly remove from the heat. Squeeze out the excess water from the gelatine leaves and stir them into the creamy mixture. Leave to cool and infuse for about 5 minutes, then remove the lime leaves and pour into six 6cm (2½-inch) diameter dariole moulds. Refrigerate for at least 6 hours, or overnight.

For the sesame honeycomb, line a small loaf tin (pan) with baking parchment. Put the sugar and syrup into a small, deep pan over a gentle heat and heat until the sugar has melted. Once completely melted, turn up the heat a little and simmer until you have an amber-coloured caramel (this will happen quickly so keep an eye on it), then immediately remove from the heat. Add the bicarbonate of soda and beat it in with a wooden spoon until it has all disappeared and the mixture is foaming. Immediately tip into the lined tin, taking care as the mixture will be very hot. Quickly sprinkle over the sesame seeds and leave to cool for at least 2 hours. You can then break it into smaller chunks. The honeycomb will keep in an airtight container for a week.

To plate up, dip the base of each panna cotta dariole mould in just-boiled water for 2 seconds, then turn out onto a shallow bowl or plate. Scoop over the pulp of half a passionfuit and place a few chunks of honeycomb on top. Decorate with a few sprigs of Thai basil cress or leaves.

papaya pavlova

Pavlova is always a dinner-party showstopper. Once you master the base, the canvas is there to be painted with seasonal fruit, ice cream and chocolate. This is inspired by my breakfast memories in Thailand, where they serve papaya with a wedge of lime; I love the fresh squeeze of citrus against the soft, perfumed, sunset flesh. I use fresh lime leaf here to intensify the citrus notes, but if you can't find it then lime zest and mint will work well. This has it all: texture, sweetness, creaminess and exotic fruit to transport you to a faraway beach hideaway.

The base will keep for up to 3 days in an airtight container, and the cream can be whipped an hour in advance and stored in the fridge. You can also use shop-bought meringues; as always, no judgement here, but you will miss out on the squidginess of a fresh meringue.

Serves 6

For the meringue base
4 egg whites
Pinch of sea salt
½ tsp lemon juice (or white wine
   vinegar)
225g (8oz) caster (superfine) sugar

For the lime-infused papaya
Juice of 1 lime
2 large firm papayas, peeled and sliced
   (or 1 large mango)
3 large fresh makrut lime leaves,
   shredded (or mint)

For the whipped cream
250ml (8fl oz) double (heavy) cream
   (or 350ml/12fl oz and don't use
   crème fraîche or yogurt)
100ml (3½fl oz) crème fraîche or
   Greek yogurt
20g (¾oz) icing (confectioners') sugar
1 tsp vanilla bean paste

To finish
Lime zest
Toasted coconut flakes and edible
   violas (optional)

Preheat the oven to 140°C/275°F/gas mark 1 and line a baking tray with baking parchment.

Whisk the egg whites in a clean, dry bowl until frothy, then add the salt, lemon juice (or vinegar) and whisk to soft peaks. Whisk in the sugar a spoonful at a time until the mixture is thick and glossy. Ensure the sugar has all dissolved by feeling between your fingers; if not, continue to whisk for another minute or two.

Dab a little mixture on the underside of the baking parchment to stick it down to the baking tray. Spoon the meringue mixture into the centre of the parchment, using the back of the spoon to create one large round, 20–23cm (8–9 inches) in diameter with a slightly raised ridge around the edge. Transfer to the oven, immediately reduce the temperature to 120°C/250°F/gas mark ½ and cook for 1 hour 15 minutes, then turn off the oven and leave the meringue inside to cool for at least an hour.

Meanwhile, in a bowl, squeeze the lime over the sliced papaya (or mango) and add half the shredded lime leaves (or mint).

Whip the cream, crème fraîche (or yogurt), icing sugar and vanilla to stiff peaks.

To assemble, spoon the whipped cream over the cooled meringue base, arrange the papaya over the top, grate over some lime zest and sprinkle over the remaining lime leaves (or mint). Some toasted coconut flakes and violas will make the pavlova super-pretty, and extra-fancy.

tahini & chocolate chunk cookies

The addition of tahini and sea salt makes these cookies so sophisticated, but let's be childish and sandwich ice cream between them… Any ice cream is fine but I particularly like this with the miso ice cream on page 163. You can substitute tahini for any nut butter, but tahini's sesame hit is so moreish and adds a real depth of flavour. The dough is lovely if left overnight (but also fine if chilled for an hour), making a great get-ahead recipe. You can then serve the cookies warm to your guests, or bake and keep in an airtight container.

Makes 12–15

140g (5oz) unsalted butter (or coconut oil), softened
100g (3½oz) tahini, stirred well
1 tsp vanilla extract
140g (5oz) soft dark brown sugar
100g (3½oz) granulated sugar
1 large egg
150g (5oz) plain (all-purpose) flour
1 tsp baking powder
½ tsp bicarbonate of soda (baking soda)
1 tsp flaky sea salt
150g (5¼oz) dark chocolate, chopped into large chunks
White sesame seeds (optional)

Cream together the butter (or coconut oil), tahini, vanilla and sugars until pale but not fluffy. You can do this with a wooden spoon or in a stand mixer with the paddle attachment. Next, add in the egg and beat until combined.

Now mix together the dry ingredients and fold them into the butter mixture, along with the chocolate chunks.

Divide into 50g (1¾oz) balls and place on a lined baking tray. Cover with cling film (plastic wrap) and refrigerate for at least 6 hours, or overnight.

When ready to bake, preheat the oven to 180°C/350°F/gas mark 4.

Press each ball down slightly to flatten and sprinkle over some sesame seeds. Ensure the dough balls are evenly spaced with room to spread (you may need a second baking tray, or to bake them in batches) and bake for 13 minutes. Remove from the oven and leave to cool on the tray; they may appear slightly underdone in the middle, but they will firm up as they cool.

Eat slightly warm with a cup of coffee, or sandwich with ice cream. Keep a few aside in a tin for moments of calm; they will keep well for up to 3 days.

piña colada tarte tatin

A tarte Tatin is an elegant French institution where people will think your pastry skills are off the scale, but it's actually such a simple dessert to pull off, and a few shop-bought ingredients will transport you to the tropics. Infused with rum and served with coconut ice cream, this make-ahead dessert never fails to impress at a dinner party. To make it vegan, simply use a butter substitute.

Serves 4–6

100g (3½oz) golden caster (superfine) sugar
25g (1oz) butter
3 star anise
2 tbsp Malibu (optional)
100g (3½oz) canned pineapple rings (or fresh), patted dry
1 x 320g (11½oz) sheet of puff pastry
Toasted coconut flakes, to decorate
Coconut ice cream (see page 162 for homemade), to serve

Preheat the oven to 200°C/400°F/gas mark 6.

Sprinkle the sugar into a wide, ovenproof frying pan, place over a low–medium heat and melt to a caramel colour. Add the butter, star anise and Malibu (if using) and cook, swirling, until combined. Add the pineapple rings and turn to coat them in the caramel before arranging in a single layer across the pan.

Cut out a circle from the pastry the diameter of your frying pan and cover the pineapples with the pastry, tucking the edges under around the edges. (You can also make individual tarts; simply use a cookie cutter for discs of pastry, place the pineapple and caramel in individual tart cases and follow the tucking in method, baking for 15–18 minutes.)

Bake in the oven for 18–20 minutes until the pastry is risen and golden. Remove from the oven and leave to stand for 5 minutes before turning out onto a plate, pineapple side up.

Sprinkle with toasted coconut flakes and cut into slices to serve with coconut ice cream.

cardamom & chocolate orange tea cups

Probably the best desserts for entertaining are those you can make a few days ahead that can then happily chill in the fridge until you need them. Always a winner when you need a chocolate hit and the coconut milk is so rich and creamy. If you have guests who are vegan or lactose intolerant, use dairy-free chocolate for a plant-based version; it saves you making two puddings.

The slight perfume from the cardamom keeps it sophisticated and, well, orange is always best chums with chocolate! It's also so versatile – decorate with any crumbly cookies, honeycomb, nutty granola or berries. This is one the easiest puddings you will ever make, fact.

Serves 6

1 x 400g (14oz) can of full-fat coconut milk (ideally at least 70% coconut extract)
150g (5¼oz) dark cooking chocolate (at least 60% cocoa solids), broken into pieces
150g (5¼oz) milk chocolate, broken into pieces
½ tsp ground cardamom (ground seeds from 3 pods)
½ tsp vanilla bean paste
Grated zest of 1 orange
Pinch of flaky sea salt
Crushed cookies, honeycomb, nutty granola, berries or mint leaves, to garnish (optional)

Heat the coconut milk in a saucepan over medium heat, whisking it for a couple of minutes until it begins to steam. Remove from the heat, add both chocolates, the cardamom, vanilla, orange zest and salt. Gently whisk until combined and smooth, and the chocolate has melted, then set aside to cool for at least 10 minutes.

Pour the mixture into individual tea cups and refrigerate for at least 4 hours until set. Garnish with your favourite topping, if you like.

cheat's cappuccino brioche with gelato

It's okay to cheat sometimes, especially when you've made everything else from scratch; convenience is your friend! This ice-cream sandwich is a portable breakfast in Sicily to cool down commuters. I totally love it – it's the perfect dessert for me, and the coffee ice cream is a delicious pick-me-up. The fun element will delight your guests and they will appreciate the ease of this pudding because they can replicate it when they host dinner parties!

Serves 4

1 tub of shop-bought coffee ice cream
  (or a flavour of your choice)
4 brioche buns, sliced in half
A little butter (optional)
About 4 tbsp Nutella
50g (1¾oz) crushed roasted hazelnuts
  or pecans

Remove the ice cream from the freezer, and lightly toast your brioche buns in a toaster or pan. I prefer toasting on a pan by spreading a little butter on the cut sides and cooking cut-side down until golden brown. This will prevent the brioche going soggy and give a lovely crisp texture.

Spread the bottom side of each brioche with about 1 tablespoon of Nutella. Place 1 or 2 scoops of coffee ice cream in the bun, top with the crushed nuts and gently squish down with the top brioche halves. Serve with a napkin and optional teaspoon!

brown butter madeleines
& pomegranate glaze

These oyster-shaped cakes are the easiest, prettiest little cakes you can ever make; the tin does all the hard work for you. Once you master the sponge, the creativity opportunities are endless. A dusting of icing sugar is also magic, but elevating them with a glaze makes them French-patisserie-window worthy.

I've added a Middle Eastern influence with the pomegranate glaze, for a pretty pink tone, and with the rose petals and pistachios this delicious delight will have your guests taking photos for the Gram! The brown butter gives these morsels more depth and luxury.

Makes 16–18

100g (3½oz) unsalted butter, plus extra, melted, for greasing
100g (3½oz) plain (all-purpose) flour, plus extra for dusting
1 tsp baking powder
Pinch of sea salt
2 eggs
100g (3½oz) caster (superfine) sugar
1 tbsp clear honey
1 tsp vanilla bean paste
20ml (¾fl oz) slightly warm milk

For the pomegranate glaze
50g (1¾oz) icing (confectioners') sugar
1 tsp pomegranate molasses
4 tsp water

To garnish
Edible rose petals
Sliced pistachios

Put the butter in a light-coloured pan so you can see it changing colour, place over a medium heat, then simmer for 4–5 minutes until it turns golden brown. Once the butter starts to foam, keep your eyes on it because it can go from brown to burnt very quickly. Pour into a heatproof bowl and set aside to cool.

Mix the flour, baking powder and salt together in a small bowl. In a separate, large bowl and using an electric beater, whisk the eggs, sugar, honey and vanilla for about 5 minutes, until fluffy. Gradually whisk in the dry ingredients, followed by the cooled melted butter and the milk. Cover and chill for about 2 hours, or overnight.

Grease a madeleine mould well with melted butter and lightly dust with flour, tipping out any excess. If you only have one mould you might need to bake the madeleines in 2 batches, depending on the size of your mould. Leave this in the fridge for 15 minutes while you prepare the glaze by mixing the ingredients together; you want the consistency of double cream.

Preheat the oven to 200°C/400°F/gas mark 6.

Spoon 1 level tablespoon of the madeleine mixture into each dip in the prepared mould and bake for about 8–10 minutes until golden. Tip the madeleines gently onto a wire rack to cool for about 10 minutes, while you bake the next batch.

Decorate the cooled madeleines by dipping half of each in the pomegranate glaze. Sprinkle with rose petals and pistachios, and serve on the same day. I love these with a cup of fresh mint tea.

grilled amaretto peaches with whipped amaretti mascarpone

This is the perfect dinner-party dessert. No baking, a throw-together low-effort, last-minute pudding. Grilling fruit intensifies the flavour, and soaking in alcohol gives you an instant sauce, although you can skip it – or use almond syrup – if you prefer to keep this booze-free. The separate components can be made ahead of time; however, I do recommend grilling the peaches when you are ready to serve, as the contrast of warm and cold is divine.

Serves 4

4 firm peaches
8 shop-bought amaretti biscuits, slightly crushed
Finely shredded mint leaves, to decorate

For the poaching syrup
200ml (7fl oz) water
100ml (3½fl oz) Amaretto liqueur (or almond syrup)
50g (1¾oz) caster (superfine) sugar
4 pared strips of lemon zest
Juice of ½ lemon
1 vanilla pod (bean) or ½ tsp vanilla bean paste

For the whipped mascarpone
250g (9oz) mascarpone, at room temperature
200ml (7fl oz) double (heavy) cream
50g (1¾oz) icing (confectioners') sugar
Seeds from 1 vanilla pod (see poaching syrup above) or 1 tsp vanilla bean paste

First make the poaching syrup by combining the water, Amaretto (or almond syrup), sugar, lemon zest strips and lemon juice in a pan. If using a vanilla pod, split it in half lengthways and scrape out the seeds. Set the seeds aside to use in the cream and add the empty pod to the poaching syrup pan (or the vanilla bean paste). Gently bring to the boil, then turn down the heat and simmer for 5 minutes until the sugar has dissolved. Take off the heat and leave to cool to room temperature.

Halve the peaches and remove the stones (pits), place in a baking tray or dish cut-side up and pour over the cooled poaching syrup. Leave to soak for at least 1 hour, turning them once halfway.

Next, whip the mascarpone, cream, icing sugar and reserved vanilla seeds (or paste, if using) together, using an electric whisk or by hand, until light and fluffy.

Heat a griddle pan, ideally non-stick, over a medium-high heat until hot, place the peaches cut-side down in the pan. Leave for about 2 minutes to achieve the blackened griddle marks, then turn them over and cook for an extra minute on the other side.

Reduce the poaching syrup by simmering for 10 minutes. When ready to plate, you can present on one large sharing platter or as individual servings. Swirl the whipped mascarpone onto your chosen base, place 2 peach halves on top, drizzle over the poaching syrup, generously sprinkle over the crushed amaretti and decorate with mint leaves.

kataifi pistachio cheesecake with berries

When eating out, I will never order cheesecake. For me, it's too dense and that biscuit base is uninspiring. But my mind was blown when I tried a Middle Eastern cheesecake at London's Honey & Co. The main difference is the kataifi – pastry base. Kataifi is thread-like filo (phyllo) noodles which are very popular in Greek and Levantine sweet treats. You can find it in the freezer section of Middle Eastern stores, or online, or use a knife or scissors to cut up filo pastry; it won't be the same, but is close enough.

These little pastry nests topped with a cheese mixture, fruit and nuts are almost the lost connection between baklava and cheesecake. Taking inspiration from that magnificent dessert experience, I'm replacing the feta with mascarpone, and adding pistachio paste and a fruity molasses. The berries add freshness, but seasonal cherries or pomegranate would be beautiful too. It is the perfect make-ahead dessert for entertaining.

Serves 4

For the pastry bases
25g (1oz) unsalted butter, diced
100g (3½oz) kataifi pastry
2 tbsp caster (superfine) sugar

For the cheesecake pistachio cream
150g (5¼oz) cream cheese
150g (5¼oz) extra thick double
　(heavy) cream
40g (1½oz) runny honey
50g (2oz) mascarpone
1 tsp vanilla bean paste or seeds from
　½ vanilla pod (bean)
40g (1½oz) pistachio paste/butter
　(shop-bought)

To finish
Blueberries and blackberries, some
　halved (cherries and pomegranate
　also work)
Mixed nuts, such as almonds and
　walnuts, chopped
Toasted pistachios, finely chopped
Runny honey and sour cherry molasses
　(or pomegranate molasses)
Edible pink dianthus flowers, or dried
　edible rose petals
Micro mint or lemon balm

Preheat the oven to 180°C/350°F/gas mark 4.

Melt the butter for the pastry cases and leave to cool slightly.

In a wide tray, separate the pastry slightly, pour over the melted butter and sprinkle over the sugar. Mix together well then create 4 little nests using equal amounts of pastry. Place on a baking tray and cook for 12–15 minutes until golden. Remove from the oven and leave to cool. They will keep for 2–3 days in an airtight container, so you can prepare them in advance.

Next, place all the cheesecake cream ingredients except the pistachio paste in a bowl. Whip by hand for 2–3 minutes, folding the mixture until it is combined and thick, then fold in the pistachio paste.

When ready to serve, spoon the cheesecake mixture onto the pastry nests and top with fruit and chopped nuts. Drizzle the honey and molasses around the plate, and finish with a sprinkling of pistachios, edible flowers or dried rose petals and mint or lemon balm.

palate cleansers

As part of my dining experience, I always serve a refreshing palate cleanser to split the starter from the main course. This resets the taste buds to allow the brain to start again and appreciate the new flavours which will be introduced. My dining experiences can be up to 10 courses, so that's why I feel this reset is necessary. By all means use these ideas as a little pre-dessert, or an actual dessert, for a refreshing ending.

I serve my palate cleaners as a granita, sorbet or a fun lolly (popsicle). Depends on my mood and the season! The mini lolly moulds can be found online.

Granita
Granita originates from Italy. It is a handmade variation of sorbet where you flake the ice every few hours to achieve a coarse, snow-like flaky texture instead of a smooth sorbet, which usually requires a machine.

Granita method
If using fresh fruit, first blitz it in a blender. Combine the ingredients in a measuring jug (pitcher). Pour into a medium-sized plastic tub. Freeze, uncovered, for 1 hour, then remove and start scraping with a fork to break up the ice crystals. Freeze for a further hour and rake the crystals again; you should achieve larger crystals. This process needs to be repeated twice and the granita should be left to freeze for a total of 3 hours.

Sorbet and lolly method
Sorbet is a great refreshing palate cleanser or dessert. Also a wonderful vegan alternative to ice cream if you are avoiding dairy. Add any fruit or liquid to a smoothie blender and blitz until smooth. Set in a silicone mould with lolly sticks or in a freezable container. Freeze overnight and scoop out when needed. For super-smooth sorbet, churn the mixtures overleaf in an ice-cream machine on the sorbet setting.

{recipes overleaf}

orange & aperol granita or sorbet

Serves 6

250ml (8fl oz) freshly squeezed
   orange juice
40g (1¾oz) caster (superfine) sugar
120ml (4fl oz/½ cup) Aperol
1 tsp lemon juice
Mint leaves, to garnish

Simmer the orange juice and sugar for 3–4 minutes until the sugar is dissolved. Leave to cool then add the Aperol and lemon juice. Follow the granita method on page 159. Alternatively, for a sorbet, set into a mould without flaking every few hours. Churning in an ice-cream machine before setting in a mould will result in a smoother sorbet. Garnish with mint leaves.

passionfruit & coconut snow

Serves 6

75g (2½oz) caster (superfine) sugar
240ml (8fl oz/1 cup) coconut water
1 lime leaf
6 passionfruit, pulp scraped out
   (do not blitz)

In a pan, simmer the sugar and coconut water with the lime leaf for 3–4 minutes until the sugar has melted. Remove the lime leaf and add the passionfruit juice (strain through a small sieve/strainer, reserving the seeds). Follow the granita method on page 159. Scoop out into small glasses when ready to serve and garnish with the passionfruit seeds.

melon & thai basil flaked ice

Serves 6

1 cantaloupe melon, flesh cubed
25g (1oz) Thai basil leaves
Juice of 1 lime
100g (3½oz) icing (confectioners') sugar

Blitz all the ingredients in a processor until smooth. Transfer to an ice-cream machine to churn into a sorbet, or follow the granita method on page 159 for flaked ice.

pineapple & mint granita

Serves 6

1 pineapple (about 500g/1lb 2oz), cored
   and roughly chopped
100g (3½oz) caster (superfine) sugar
20g (¾oz) mint leaves
Grated zest and juice of 2 limes, plus
   extra zest to serve

Blitz everything together until smooth, then follow the granita method on page 159. Serve with extra lime zest on top.

lychee & lemongrass sorbet

Serves 6

2 x 400g (14oz) cans of lychees in syrup
30g (1oz) caster (superfine) sugar
1 lemongrass stalk, bashed
Zest of 2 limes, juice of 1 lime
Dried rose petals, to decorate (optional)

Drain the lychee syrup into a pan and add the sugar and lemongrass. Bring to the boil, then boil for 1 minute. Let cool to room temperature, remove the lemongrass and add the syrup to a blender with the lychees and lime zest and juice. Set in a mould or a tub and freeze overnight. (For a super smooth sorbet, I like to churn this mixture in my Magimix Gelato Expert before filling the mould.) Decorate with dried rose petals, if you like.

lime leaf sherbet

1 tbsp caster (superfine) sugar
1 tsp lime zest
Finely blitzed lime leaf (optional)

Adding this zesty sherbet to any of the above granitas or sorbets gives a lovely finish.

Mix the ingredients together to achieve a zesty sherbet, then sprinkle on top of any sorbet or granita.

effortless ice creams

Ice creams are so simple and cost effective to make at home, but often we buy them for convenience. Master my three-ingredient ice creams, with or without an ice-cream machine (I like to use my Magimix Gelato Expert), and the combinations are endless. I make the below three flavours because you can't find them easily in the shops, and also they are very Asian-influenced and marry well with my recipes.

coconut ice cream *(dairy-free)*

Serves 8

1 x 400g (14oz) can of full-fat
   coconut milk
300ml (10fl oz/1¼ cups) coconut cream
225g (8oz) caster (superfine) sugar
4 tbsp water
Generous pinch of sea salt

In a large jug (pitcher), whisk together the coconut milk and cream. Set aside.

In a small pan, heat the sugar and water gently over a medium heat until dissolved and slightly thick. Pour the sugar syrup into the coconut mixture, add the salt, mix, cover with cling film (plastic wrap) and refrigerate for 2 hours.

Either churn in an ice-cream machine or freeze in a shallow plastic or metal tub for 1 hour, then whisk thoroughly to break up the ice crystals. Repeat once more, then for the final time blend in a food processor until combined before returning to the freezer for 5 hours or overnight.

Remove from the fridge 5–10 minutes before serving.

This ice cream is delicious alone or with the piña colada tarte Tatin on page 149. It's also good with chocolate sauce and chopped nuts, or some mango purée and coconut flakes.

matcha ice cream *(no-churn method)*

I first saw this idea on the BBC's *Simply Nigella* show and I've been
making a version of it ever since.

Serves 6

150ml (5fl oz) condensed milk
300ml (10fl oz/1¼ cups) double
  (heavy) cream
30g (1oz) matcha green tea powder
1 tsp vanilla extract (optional)

Put the condensed milk in a bowl and use a balloon whisk to
loosen it until creamy. Add the cream and whip together until
thick. Add the matcha powder, and vanilla if using, and mix
until combined.

Decant into a freezer container, about 1 litre (34fl oz/4 cups).

Freeze overnight, then serve as it is, or with the the tahini
chocolate chunk cookies on page 148.

cheat's miso ice cream

Serves 4

500g (1lb 2oz) vanilla ice cream
  (shop-bought)
1 tbsp white miso
50g (1¾oz) honey

Take the ice cream out of the freezer and leave at room
temperature for 10 minutes. In a bowl, mix together the miso
and honey. Pour this over the ice cream and swirl it through.
Freeze for at least 3 hours before using. Perfect sandwiched
between the tahini chocolate chunk cookies (page 148), for a
fun dessert.

strawberry &
lemongrass posset

I've been inspired by the quintessential British summer drink Pimm's and
lemonade. The zingy lemon base, with Pimm's-infused strawberries and
mint, is a refreshing way to end a meal. To add an Asian accent, I infuse
the base with lemongrass. You can top with any fruits, and defrosted frozen
mixed berries also work well here – with a lemon posset, the possibilities
are endless. A perfect make-ahead pudding that will sit happily in the
fridge for up to 3 days.

Serves 6

300g (10½oz) strawberries, sliced
  or quartered
50ml (2fl oz) Pimm's (or 1 tbsp aged
  balsamic vinegar)
Micro mint/lemon balm or edible
  flowers, to decorate (optional)

For the lemon posset
600ml (20fl oz/2½ cups) double
  (heavy) cream
200g (7oz) golden caster (superfine)
  sugar
2 lemongrass stalks, bashed
Grated zest of 3 lemons, plus 75ml
  (5 tbsp) juice

For the shortbread (makes about 20)
100g (3½oz) plain (all-purpose) flour
50g (2oz) icing (confectioners') sugar
¼ tsp ground cinnamon
Pinch of sea salt
75g (2½oz) butter, cut into small cubes
1 egg yolk

For the posset, put the cream, sugar and lemongrass into a large
pan, place over a low heat and gently warm, stirring, until the
sugar has dissolved. Bring to a simmer and bubble for 1 minute,
then take off the heat and stir in the lemon zest and juice.
Remove and discard the lemongrass. Divide the mixture between
individual cups or bowls, or pour into a deep serving dish. Cool
to room temperature, then refrigerate for at least 4 hours, or
ideally overnight.

To make the shortbread, combine the flour, icing sugar,
cinnamon and salt in a bowl. Add the butter and rub it in using
your fingertips, until you achieve a sandy consistency. Add
the egg yolk, mix with a fork, then use your hands to bring it
together into a dough. Halve the dough, take one ball and flatten
between 2 sheets of baking parchment. Roll out with a rolling
pin as thinly as possible. Repeat with the remaining dough, and
refrigerate for at least 15 minutes, or until ready to use.

Preheat the oven to 180°C/350°F/gas mark 4 and line 2 baking
trays with baking parchment.

Remove the dough from the fridge and use a small (5cm/2-inch)
plain cookie cutter to cut out rounds. Place on the lined baking
trays and bake in the oven for 7–8 minutes, until pale brown.
Remove and leave to cool on the trays. These will keep for
3 days in an airtight container.

Put the strawberries in a bowl, pour over the Pimm's (or
balsamic) and leave to macerate for about 15 minutes.

To serve, top the possets with the strawberries, pour over some
of the syrup, decorate with the mint, lemon balm or edible
flowers, if using, and serve with some of the shortbread.

cocktails & mocktails

Set the tone for your dinner party with seasonal welcome cocktails. There is also nothing wrong with serving a glass of fizz or elderflower spritz with a strawberry garnish when your friends walk through the door. This is me being extra over the top – to make your guests feel super-special.

lychee martini

A favourite of mine with Asian canapés.

Serves 1

25ml (5 tsp/1fl oz) gin
25ml (5 tsp/1fl oz) lychee liqueur
5ml (1 tsp) lime juice
75ml (5 tbsp) lychee juice
Rose bud/petal or a fresh lychee,
   to garnish

Add cubed ice to a shaker with all the liquid ingredients and shake for 10–12 seconds. Double-strain into a coupe glass and garnish with a rose bud, petal or a fresh lychee.

guava colada

A Thai-inspired refreshing cocktail. For a mocktail version, omit the rum.

Serves 1

50ml (2fl oz) rum (optional)
10ml (2 tsp) lime juice
30ml (2 tbsp) coconut water
70ml (2½fl oz) guava juice
2 fresh lime leaves, stems removed
4 ice cubes

To garnish
1 lime leaf
Wedge of lime

Add all the ingredients to a cocktail shaker and shake well for about 30 seconds. Pour into a glass and garnish with a lime leaf and wedge of lime. You can also make this cocktail without a cocktail shaker, simply by mixing together in a jug (pitcher).

watermelon daiquiri

Perfect for summer.

Serves 1

200g (7oz) peeled watermelon,
    plus 4 wedges, to garnish
45ml (3 tbsp) superior white rum
Juice of ½ lime
1 tsp caster (superfine) sugar
2 ice cubes

Blitz all the ingredients in a blender and serve in a glass with a watermelon garnish.

elderflower & lemongrass smash

For a mocktail, omit the gin.

Serves 1

1 lemongrass stalk
30ml (2 tbsp) gin
Juice of ½ lemon
45ml (3 tbsp) elderflower cordial
Soda water, to top up
Cucumber ribbons, to garnish

Bash the lemongrass with a rolling pin and add to a tall glass, with ice. Pour in the measure of gin, then the lemon juice and elderflower cordial. Top up with soda water, stir well with the lemongrass and garnish with cucumber ribbons.

mango bellini

A tropical twist on a classic Bellini.

Serves 1

30ml (2 tbsp) mango purée
Prosecco or Champagne, to top up
1 raspberry, to garnish

Add the purée to a Champagne flute, top up with fizz and garnish with a raspberry.

passionfruit punch

Exotic with a playful character.

Serves 1

35ml (1¼fl oz) vodka
15ml (1 tbsp) Passoã liqueur
10ml (2 tsp) lime juice
10ml (2 tsp) vanilla syrup
75ml (5 tbsp) passionfruit juice
1 passionfruit, halved, to garnish

Add cubed ice to a shaker with all the liquid ingredients and shake for 10–12 seconds. Double-strain into a coupe glass and garnish with half a passionfruit.

pineapple mojito

Beach vibes with this Cuban classic. For a mocktail version, omit the rum.

Serves 1

10 mint leaves, plus a mint sprig
   to garnish
1 tbsp white sugar
1 tbsp fresh pineapple cubes
170ml (5¾fl oz) pineapple juice
50ml (5fl oz) rum
Splash of soda water
1 wedge of fresh pineapple, to garnish

Muddle the mint leaves, sugar and pineapple in a highball glass. Fill the glass with ice cubes. Pour in the pineapple juice and rum. Top with a splash of soda water and garnish with the pineapple wedge and mint sprig.

classic aperol spritz

Officially the best aperitif to ever exist, in my humble opinion! Venice vibes with this drink that increases your appetite!

Serves 2

100ml (3½fl oz) Aperol
150ml (5fl oz) Prosecco
Soda, to top up
2 orange slices, to garnish

Divide the Aperol between 2 glasses with ice. Divide the Prosecco between the glasses then top up with soda and garnish with orange slices.

sides, chutneys & pantry

To dress, drizzle and dunk – everything tastes better with a side and chutneys. Use this section to elevate your dishes and create your own flavour combinations. And don't restrict your choice of accompaniment to the dishes I have suggested; they are intended to be woven into all of your cooking as you become familiar with the ingredients and their flavour profiles.

Some people get excited about walk-in wardrobes, I get excited about walk-in pantries! While I don't have enough space to house one, I have plenty of cupboards and drawers dedicated to cans and condiments. With shelves groaning under the weight of flours, lentils, beans, tomatoes, pastes, pastas, rice and noodles, all towering together with bottles of soy sauce, oils and vinegars, I think I could survive on pantry meals alone for at least a few weeks. In fact, some of my best inventions have been created from pantry raids.

Here are some of my favourite sides and store-cupboard ingredients that will help enhance your cooking and impress your guests with ease.

green coconut sambal

A gorgeous sambal with texture, earthy depth, zesty tones and sweetness from the coconut. I had this in Malaysia, where they use fresh coconut, and by all means use fresh if you can get hold of it. This is more of an accessible recipe using desiccated coconut, which is a brilliant store-cupboard essential for sweet and savoury recipes. I like the green vibrancy from the green chilli, but feel free to use red. Serve with curries, daals, roast meats and fish. It provides a beautiful freshness with heat.

Serves 4

150g (5¼oz) desiccated (dried shredded) coconut
Small handful (about 20g/¾oz) of coriander (cilantro), including stems
1 green finger chilli, or 2 for extra spice
1 small garlic clove, peeled
Juice of 1 lime
1 tbsp olive oil
Splash of water
Sea salt, to taste

Blitz all the ingredients together in a small food processor to form a paste, still retaining some texture. Rest for at least 15 minutes before serving. This keeps well in the fridge overnight, but bring it to room temperature to serve.

tomato & chilli sambal

Sambal simply means chilli sauce, and this is so addictive. This recipe originates from Indonesia, where it is a versatile chilli sauce for chicken, rice dishes, for dipping or for eggs. You can also use this mixed with coconut milk for a curry sauce.

Serves 2–4

5 large red chillies (or 3 bird's eye)
2 vine tomatoes
2 shallots (or ½ onion), peeled
3 small garlic cloves, peeled
Thumb-sized piece of fresh ginger, peeled
3 fresh makrut lime leaves
½ tsp ground turmeric
½ tsp coriander seeds
1 tsp palm sugar or white sugar
½ tsp sea salt
Juice of 1 lime
1 tbsp virgin coconut oil

Blitz all the ingredients except the oil to a fine paste in a food processor. Heat the coconut oil in a pan over a low heat, carefully tip in the paste (it will splatter) and simmer for 5 minutes. That's it! It keeps for 3 days in the fridge.

two-ingredient naan

Flour and yogurt. That's all.

These are the only ingredients you need to make this naan that sent my Instagram and YouTube crazy over lockdown. Absolutely everyone was making them! The ease and the perfect results every time make this great for scooping up your curries, wrapping kebabs or dunking into hummus. This chewy, versatile flatbread will leave you feeling very smug!

Makes 10

275g (10oz) self-raising flour, plus
  extra for dusting
250g (9oz) Greek yogurt (or plain
  yogurt)
¼ tsp sea salt (I do not count salt as
  an ingredient!)

To finish (optional)
Butter
Coriander (cilantro) leaves

In a large mixing bowl, combine the flour, yogurt and salt using a fork, until you get big clumps. Knead with your hands for at least 5 minutes until you get a cohesive dough. The more you knead, the less sticky it will be. Cover and let the dough rest for at least 15 minutes.

Now get ready to roll out on a floured surface; don't worry about perfect round naans, they are supposed to be irregular in shape. Rip off a piece of dough, 50g (1¾oz) if you want to be precise. Roll it out into an oval; the dough will be quite stretchy and come back on itself, but persevere.

Heat a non-stick frying pan and add the rolled-out naan. Cook for about 10 seconds until you see little bubbles forming, then quickly flip over to cook the other side. Flip over a final time and gently press down with a spatula until you achieve some nice brown spots. Do not flip more than 3 times. Remove from the pan and slather in butter, if you like. Serve sprinkled with coriander, if desired. Repeat with the remaining dough.

Make ahead
Make these a few hours in advance and store wrapped in a tea towel or in an airtight container. Reheat in a dry pan when ready to eat. However, they are best eaten fresh.

chapatis – gujarati-style rotli

The fabric of India is held together with the threads of chapati, the quintessential bread for scooping up curries and daal. Learning the art of 'rotli' was a rite of passage for my mum. As a child I moaned and whined about helping her make them when all I wanted to do was watch TV, but I am now so thankful to her for persevering and teaching me the ritual of chapati making – it's heartwarming to see the generational bonds that are forged through something as simple as making bread. Now my son has started to take an interest, and, like me, he has climbed the ranks from butter spreader, to mixing the dough, making the dough balls, kneading… and is slowly on his way to graduating with the round rotli rolling degree.

Makes about 12–14

1 tbsp oil (sunflower or rapeseed/ canola), plus an extra drizzle
300g (10½oz) chapati flour, plus a small bowl (about 100g/3½oz) for dusting
200ml (7fl oz) just-boiled water

In a large mixing bowl, mix the oil into the flour with a fork until incorporated and you have a sand-like texture. Add half the water and continue to combine with the fork, then add the rest of the water and keep mixing together. When it's warm enough to handle, knead the dough really well with your knuckles, ensuring the bowl is wiped clean as you knead. Drizzle in a drop of oil, knead again and leave to rest for at least 10 minutes.

Now break off equal-sized pieces of dough. In the palm of your hands, roll a piece into the perfect ball and squash flat. Dip into the bowl of chapati flour and roll out until about 8cm (3¼ inches) in diameter. Dip again into the flour and roll out once more until you have a thin disc about 20cm (8 inches) across. (The technique to rolling round chapatis takes years of practice – the idea is to encourage the chapati to turn clockwise as you roll, without applying too much pressure. I have a YouTube video if you need help with this technique.)

Heat a dry flat frying pan over a medium heat for at least 3 minutes. (I would suggest rolling out 3 or 4 chapatis at a time, to have them ready to cook. Once you become more confident you can simultaneously roll while the chapatis cook.) Place a chapati into the pan, then, after 10 seconds, using tongs, flip the chapati over and cook on the other side for about 30 seconds. Try not to move or press the chapati, as you want small air bubbles to form. Flip over for a final time, then gently press down on the chapati using a spatula; it will start to puff up. You want to aim for golden brown cheetah-like spots on the surface of the bread. Gently remove each chapati and wrap in a tea towel to keep warm and soft, or place in a chapati container, while you cook the rest.

bao buns

This pillowy sandwich is having its moment. I just love the way it springs
back like memory foam. You can buy them frozen, ready to steam,
from an Asian grocery store, or make your own to stuff with anything
you can dream up!

Makes about 10

375g (13¼oz) plain (all-purpose) flour,
 plus extra for dusting
1 tsp dried active yeast
1 tsp baking powder
2 tbsp caster (superfine) sugar
½ tsp sea salt
225ml (7¾fl oz) warm water
Rapeseed (canola) oil, for greasing
 and brushing

Put all the dry ingredients in a bowl and gradually add the warm
water, mixing with a fork and then going in with your hands
to create a sticky ball. Knead well on a floured surface until the
dough is smooth and bouncy. Transfer to an oiled bowl, cover
with a tea (dish) towel and leave to prove for 2 hours.

On a floured surface, knead for a minute to knock out the air,
then divide the dough into 10 equal pieces. Roll each into a
ball, then use a rolling pin to flatten each out into a circle, about
10cm (4 inches) in diameter. Brush a little oil on one side and
fold over to create a half-moon shape.

Place on a sheet of baking parchment, cover and leave for
30 minutes to plump up.

In 2 batches, place in a bamboo steamer basket with baking
parchment in the base, ensuring they are not touching, and
steam for 8–10 minutes.

Fill with the ingredients of your choice. I love filling with
Korean fried chicken, aubergine (eggplant) katsu, prawns
(shrimp) and even chicken tikka.

gyoza wrappers

Shop-bought gyoza skins and wonton wrappers are excellent; they keep for ages in your freezer and are handy for whenever you want to make dumplings. But if you do want to have a go, here is an easy three-ingredient recipe I use. You will need a pasta machine to achieve the paper-thin results. Perfect for the dumpling recipes earlier in this book.

Makes 25–30

270g (9oz) plain (all-purpose) flour,
  plus extra for dusting
½ tsp sea salt
120ml (4fl oz/½ cup) just-boiled water

Mix the ingredients together in a bowl by hand. The dough will appear flaky, but with continued kneading it will come together into a firm dough, similar to pasta. Wrap in cling film (plastic wrap) and rest for 20 minutes.

When ready to use, divide the dough in half and put each portion through a pasta machine until you get to the thinnest setting. Grab a plain cookie cutter to cut out circles and keep on a floured surface.

tomato chutney

My mum would make this for every Indian snack, full of vegetables for a complexity of flavour and the magic ingredient of tomato ketchup! It's especially good with the Maru bhajia on page 42, or any other Indian snack or some chips/crisps!

Serves 2–3

1 small carrot, peeled and roughly
  chopped
10cm (4-inch) length of cucumber,
  roughly chopped
2 vine tomatoes, roughly chopped
1 fat garlic clove, peeled
1 green finger chilli
Small bunch of coriander (cilantro)
Juice of ¼ lemon
½ tsp sugar
Sea salt, to taste
Squeeze of tomato ketchup, for colour

Put all the ingredients into a blender and pulse until smooth, but still with a chunky texture. This will keep in a glass jar for 48 hours.

addictive chilli oil

I'm having an affair with chilli oil. It's my bit on the side that I drizzle over everything from noodles to rice, dumplings and eggs. It's the melody to bring the most basic of dishes into an orchestra of theatrical drama. The most versatile condiment for everything, this chilli sauce is so addictive and essential in life! The lip-numbing effect from the Sichuan peppercorns keeps you going back for more.

I also keep a jar of Lao Gan Ma brand crispy chilli oil in my store cupboard for emergencies. It's available online and in Asian stores, but if you can't find it Chiu Chow chilli oil by Lee Kum Kee is widely available.

Makes about 300ml (10fl oz/1¼ cups)

2 tbsp Sichuan peppercorns
10 long, red dried chillies
2 tbsp Korean gochugaru chilli flakes
 (or regular chilli flakes)
1 cinnamon stick
3 star anise
300ml (10fl oz/1¼ cups) rapeseed
 (canola) oil
2 banana shallots, finely sliced
5 garlic cloves, thinly sliced
2 tsp sea salt
1 tsp caster (superfine) sugar
1 tsp light soy sauce

Toast the Sichuan peppercorns in a dry frying pan for 1 minute, then transfer to a pestle and mortar and crush to a coarse powder. Using scissors, chop up the dried chillies. Transfer to a heatproof bowl with the crushed Sichuan peppercorn, gochugaru chilli flakes, cinnamon stick and star anise.

Gently heat the oil in a pan to a low temperature and add the shallots and garlic. Cook, stirring, until slightly browned. Take off the heat and let stand for 5 minutes.

Next, carefully pour the oil over the chilli mixture in the bowl; it will sizzle. Let this infuse and cool for at least an hour.

Season with the salt, sugar and soy sauce. Discard the cinnamon stick and star anise and transfer to a screw-top jar. It will keep for 1 month in the fridge.

nuoc cham dressing

The absolute quintessential dunking, pouring, dipping sauce of Vietnamese cuisine is nuoc cham. I adore its profile and the ease of a few ingredients to create a chorus of sweet, salty, spicy and sour. It's magnificent!

Serves 2–4

Juice of 2 limes
2 tbsp water
2 tbsp fish sauce
1 tsp palm sugar or caster
   (superfine) sugar
1 lemongrass stalk, white part only,
   finely chopped (optional)
1–2 red bird's eye chillies,
   finely chopped
1 garlic clove, finely chopped

Combine the lime juice, water, fish sauce, sugar, lemongrass, chilli and garlic in a screw-top jar. Firmly secure, then shake to combine. Serve over Asian salads or as a dipping sauce for spring rolls. This will keep in the fridge for 48 hours.

ginger & garlic paste

There is one secret of Indian food. Have a batch of ginger and garlic paste pre-made, frozen and at your fingertips. This will halve your time when making Indian/Asian dishes. The shop-bought stuff isn't the same at all, so please put aside some time to make it fresh where you can. Makes all the difference.

Makes 100g (3½oz)

60g (2oz) peeled garlic cloves
40g (1¾oz) peeled fresh ginger, in cubes
Splash of water
Drizzle of oil
Pinch of sea salt

In a small food processor, blitz the ingredients together until smooth. A little bit of texture is fine.

Keep refrigerated for up to 1 week in a screw-top jar. Or freeze in a zip-lock bag, flattened. Break off little chunks as needed; it will keep well for up to 6 months.

avocado chutney

A creamy Indian take on guacamole which is so gorgeous with the crab crumpets on page 41, or anywhere you want a creamy yet spicy element.

Serves 2–3

1 large avocado, halved, pitted
   and peeled
30g (1oz) coriander (cilantro),
   leaves and stalks
1 garlic clove, peeled
2cm (¾-inch) piece of fresh ginger,
   peeled (optional)
1 green finger chilli
½ tsp ground cumin
Juice of ½ lime

Blitz the ingredients together in a blender until smooth, adding a few splashes of water to help it along if necessary.

apple chutney

I made this on MasterChef to accompany my lamb curry puffs, and the tang of the apple pairs so well with the herbs. A traditional 'chundo' that is a no-waste recipe. My grandma would make this from the apples that had fallen in the garden. Try it with parathas, samosas, curry puffs and even in sandwiches.

Serves 2–3

1 large dessert apple, cored and cut into
   chunks (skin on)
30g (1oz) coriander (cilantro), stalks
   and leaves
30g (1oz) mint leaves
2 green finger chillies
1 garlic clove, peeled
2cm (¾-inch) piece of fresh ginger,
   peeled
Juice of ½ lemon
¼ tsp sea salt
¼ tsp sugar
Splash of water

Put all the ingredients into a blender and blitz until smooth. Store in a glass jar and use within 48 hours.

beetroot raita

Just so pretty, this beetroot version gives the traditional cucumber raita a
run for its money. Perfect for any biriyani or a condiment for curry night.

Serves 2–3

2 raw beetroots (beets), peeled
    and grated
250g (9oz) plain yogurt
1 tsp cumin seeds
½ tsp mustard seeds
¼ tsp sugar
½ tsp Kashmiri chilli powder or
    cayenne pepper
Squeeze of lemon juice, to taste
Sea salt, to taste
Mint leaves, to garnish

Mix the grated beetroot with the yogurt.

In a dry frying pan, gently heat the cumin and mustard seeds
for a couple of minutes until roasted, then transfer to a mortar
and grind to a fine powder. Add this, along with the sugar, chilli
powder and salt to taste, to the raita. Squeeze in a little lemon
juice, taste, and garnish with mint leaves.

This keeps well in the fridge, covered, for up to 3 days. The
beetroot will naturally release water, but a good mix will fix this.

thai pesto

A Thai accent for this traditional Italian pesto – instead of traditional basil,
I've used Thai basil for an interesting Asian undertone.

Serves 4–6

2 bunches of Thai basil (50g/1¾oz in
    total), leaves only
2 garlic cloves, peeled
3cm (1¼-inch) piece of fresh ginger,
    peeled
2 green finger chillies
5 fresh makrut lime leaves, central
    stems removed
Juice of ½ lime
40ml (1½fl oz) olive oil
10 shelled pistachios
½ tsp sugar
10g (⅓oz) Parmesan, grated (optional)
Sea salt and ground pepper, to taste

Blitz all the ingredients together in a blender, or use a pestle and
mortar, until smooth but still with some texture. This will keep
overnight in a glass jar in the fridge.

rocket chimichurri

This recipe was born when I had a sad-looking bag of rocket in the fridge that needed using up. Usually chimichurri requires a combination of herbs, but this version is cheaper and actually tastier, with its peppery tones. Wild, unwashed rocket lasts at least 10 days in your fridge, and it's not just for salad; use it for pesto or whiz with yogurt, or use it like a herb when you don't have any! This chimichurri is perfect for grilled chicken and my harissa salmon on page 114.

Serves 4

50g (1¾oz) wild rocket (arugula), even
   on its last legs!
1 garlic clove, crushed
1 tbsp capers
1 preserved lemon, finely chopped
1 shallot, finely chopped
½ tsp Aleppo pepper (or chilli flakes)
2 tbsp white wine vinegar
¼ tsp sugar
10 tbsp extra virgin olive oil
Sea salt flakes, to taste

Finely chop the rocket leaves, taking your time and transfer to a bowl. Add the garlic, capers, preserved lemon and shallot. Add your seasonings of Aleppo pepper, vinegar, sugar and salt to taste. Add the olive oil, mix well and leave to stand for 10 minutes before serving to ensure all the flavours have infused.

This will keep in the fridge for 48 hours.

tamarind chutney

This glossy brown 'imli' chutney is the sweet-and-sour friend to most Indian street foods and essential in the beetroot bubble (see page 21). Great in chaats, bhels, salads and as a dip for pakoras or samosas. I've used the convenience of tamarind paste to save time on soaking and straining fresh tamarind fruit.

Serves 10

400ml (14fl oz) water
150g (5¼oz) jaggery or sugar
3 tbsp tamarind paste
½ tsp Kashmiri chilli powder
½ tsp ground cumin
½ tsp ground fennel
½ tsp sea salt
½ tsp salt

Put the water and jaggery or sugar into a small saucepan over a medium heat. Once the sugar has melted, stir in the tamarind paste and spices and simmer for 2–3 minutes to help the spices cook out. Take off the heat, leave to cool and serve at room temperature.

This will keep in the fridge in a sterilised glass jar for up to 1 month.

classic kachumber

I make this for a lot of my dinner parties with an Indian theme, where the freshness and crunch is essential to cut through all the complex depths of flavour. Everyone asks me for the dressing recipe – I can finally admit I cheated! It's a dollop of shop-bought mint sauce that elevates this kachumber to restaurant standard.

Serves 4

2 vine tomatoes, finely sliced
1 cucumber
1 red onion
1 tbsp shop-bought mint sauce
Sea salt, to taste
Pomegranate seeds and coriander
   (cilantro) leaves (optional, to garnish)

Sprinkle the tomato slices with salt, then set aside in a colander to drain the water.

Meanwhile, halve the cucumber lengthways and use a teaspoon to scrape out the seedy middle. Cut each half into half-moons. Finely slice the onion.

Bring everything together and mix through the mint sauce and salt to taste. It's not necessary, but if you want to be fancy, scatter over pomegranate seeds and a few coriander leaves.

coriander & mint chutney

A bright forest-green chutney which loves a samosa, chaat or any snack. Especially good in a cheese toastie!

Serves 4

100g (3½oz) coriander (cilantro),
   including stalks
25g (1oz) mint leaves
2 green finger chillies, or to taste
2 garlic cloves, peeled
2cm (¾-inch) piece of fresh
   ginger, peeled
3 tbsp lemon juice
½ tsp salt
1 tsp caster (superfine) sugar
5 tbsp water (add more if required)

Put all the ingredients, except the water, into a small blender and blend, adding the water gradually until you achieve a smooth consistency.

This will keep in the fridge in a sterilised glass jar for up to 1 month.

cardamom & cumin rice

A real staple of mine for any Indian dishes; subtle yet interesting, don't make plain rice ever again!

Serves 2

150g (5¼oz) basmati rice
½ tsp ghee or extra virgin olive oil
½ tsp cumin seeds
2 green cardamom pods
¼ tsp sea salt
300ml (10fl oz/1¼ cups) water

Soak your rice in a bowl of cold water for at least 15 minutes if you have time; this will wash out the starch and make the rice swell, reducing your cooking time. Drain all the cloudy water and rinse once. Otherwise, rinse your rice 3 times in cold running water to get rid of the cloudy starch.

In a small pan with a lid, melt the ghee or heat the oil. Add the cumin seeds and cardamom and let them sizzle for a few seconds, off the heat. Add the rice and salt and stir to coat each grain in the oil. Now add the water, bring to the boil, reduce to a simmer and pop the lid on. Cook for 10 minutes, then take off the heat and let it rest for 5 minutes to ensure all the water has been absorbed. Fluff with a fork to serve.

fragrant coconut rice

Postcard from the Far East – every Thai, Malaysian and Indonesian dish should be served with this royalty of rice. Goes especially well with the chicken rendang on page 87.

Serves 4

250g (9oz) jasmine or basmati rice
1 x 400g (14oz) can of coconut milk
¼ tsp sea salt

Place the ingredients in a pan, pop on the lid and bring to the boil. As soon as it reaches a boil, reduce the heat to a low simmer and cook for 10 minutes. Check if the rice needs any additional liquid, adding a few tablespoons of hot water if it looks dry. Cook for a further 3 minutes until all the liquid has been absorbed. Take off the heat and let the rice rest for at least 5 minutes before serving.

my pantry

Here are my store-cupboard essentials, a glossary of ingredients you may not have
come across before. All of these ingredients feature in this book and are available in
supermarkets and online.

Aleppo Pepper
Also referred to as pul biber, these aromatic chilli flakes are fruity and mild. I use
them extensively in my recipes – to infuse butter or as a garnish.

Chaat Masala
An unusual spice mix with a unique personality intertwined in Indian street food is
chaat masala. It has a pungent smell with its distinct black salt with sulphur tones,
but don't let that put you off this moreish spice mix. It typically consists of amchoor
(dried mango), cumin, coriander, ginger, salt, black pepper, asafoetida and chilli
powder. It is used as a garnish in salads like dhai puri chaat, or in cooking, such as
aloo tikki.

Chinkiang Black Vinegar
This sharp black vinegar is brewed from glutinous rice and has a complex flavour of
sweet, sour and slightly smoky. Widely available in Asian supermarkets and online.

Chilli Oil with Bits
Chilli oil is a non-negotiable condiment, but it needs to have 'bits' otherwise it's
just a light coloured spicy oil with no charisma. I want the Asian variety with crispy
garlic, shallots and the lip-numbing effect of Sichuan peppercorns. If I'm not making
my own, a back-up chilli oil in my cupboard is Lao Gan Ma or Chiu Chow, available
in supermarkets or online.

Chinese Five Spice
A brilliant store-cupboard essential and cheat: five spices blended to give a deeply
aromatic flavour. Typically these are cinnamon, black pepper, fennel seed, star anise
and cloves.

Coconut Milk
One of my favourite ingredients and flavours ever, coconut milk has the ability to
make everything luxurious. Seek out good-quality full-fat versions, ideally with at
least 70% coconut extract, to make my curries, coconut pannacotta, coconut rice
and more. I couldn't live without my little connection to tropical paradise. Favourite
brands include Chaokoh and Aroy-D, but other good-quality brands may also pass
my test.

Curry Leaves

Commonly used in Gujarati, South Indian and Sri Lankan cuisines, these weirdly smell like curry! With more of a citrusy profile, they sizzle violently when added to oil and infuse your dishes with subtle pungency. Never buy the dried version – a waste of money as they lend no flavour. They are available in supermarkets but are cheapest in Asian stores. You can buy and freeze, although fresh is best.

Dhana Jeera (ground coriander and cumin)

This is an essential blend in my spice tin. The region of India where I originate from is Gujarat, where we rely on this equal blend of ground cumin and coriander a lot in our cooking. Seek it out in Asian stores to make cooking curries a breeze.

Dried Fenugreek Leaves (Kasoori Methi)

The reason why butter chicken tastes the way it does is because of dried fenugreek leaves! Or it's at least where you may have tried this herb before. Not to be confused with fenugreek seeds, kasoori methi, as it's authentically known, is like a cross between basil, thyme and sage. Cushing between your palms over curries will release their bitter yet pungent flavour, which turns mellow and sweet once cooked out.

Dukkah

Dukkah is an Egyptian nut, seed and spice blend. The exact ingredients tend to vary, though various toasted nuts, sesame seeds, coriander and cumin are among the most common additions.

Gochujang Paste

Made from glutinous rice, fermented soy beans and chillies, this popular fermented chilli paste is used in Korean cooking. It's a spicy, sweet and savoury paste that adds a depth of flavour to your dishes. A condiment for curries, glazes, marinades, noodles, ramens… the possibilities are endless. As essential to me as ketchup! I like the O'food brand.

Harissa

Native to North Africa, this spicy chilli paste has travelled through the Middle East where it's commonly made with red chilli peppers and rose petals. A robust and versatile ingredient to marinate vegetables, meat and fish, you can make your own or use shop bought. Belazu's rose harissa is excellent and features in my aubergine tarte Tatin and harissa side of salmon.

Kashmiri Chilli Powder

My favourite red chilli powder which gives mild warmth and a fruity profile (I prefer to get my heat from fresh chillies). Kashmiri red chilli will beautifully stain your dish a deep orange but without spicy fire; perfect in my butter chicken recipe. My go-to is the Fudco brand but others are available.

Kecap Manis

An Indonesian condiment, often called 'sweet soy', this reminds me of balsamic glaze in consistency and has a sweetness like molasses from the palm sugar. I use it in stir-fries, marinades, nasi goreng, over fried eggs, sushi or just to drizzle over greens. A brilliant cousin to soy sauce when you require a sticky, salty, sweet hit. My favourite brand is ABC.

Korean Gochugaru Chilli Flakes

A Korean red pepper powder with smoky, fruity sweet notes most commonly used in Korea's national dish of kimchi. I love using these chilli flakes in my dan dan noodles, Portuguese coconut and lime chicken and in stir-fries. I like the coarse variety better than the fine.

Lemongrass

The scent of lemongrass reminds me of Thailand every time – wherever you go in Thailand, you can smell lemongrass essential oils wafting through the air. Luckily lemongrass is now available in supermarkets. The woody stalks give a complex lemony flavour essential in Thai, Malaysian, Vietnamese and Sri Lankan cooking. Can also be frozen and used as needed.

Makrut Lime Leaves

These are the Asian equivalent to bay leaves. They can be added whole to Thai curries, soups and stir-fries, then either removed or finely chopped to be eaten. You can buy them dried, but I wouldn't bother: fresh or frozen is best.

Miso Paste

Miso is a traditional Japanese seasoning, a thick paste produced by fermenting soy beans for a deep umami flavour which works in both sweet and savoury dishes. I mainly use white miso for marinades and soup bases. My favourite brand is Miso Tasty.

Nduja

Nduja is a spicy, spreadable pork sausage/chilli paste from the region of Calabria in southern Italy. There are vegan versions (vduja) available that mimic the flavour, and I particularly like the Belazu one.

Shichimi Togarashi

A Japanese blend made with chilli flakes, seaweed, sesame seeds, orange peel and ginger. Use to add colour and a fiery kick to noodle and rice dishes, sushi, soups, tempura and savoury snacks. I usually make my own or buy some from the Asian supermarket.

Sichuan Peppercorns
This glorious peppercorn smells like grapefruit and isn't spicy. It's a key ingredient in Sichuan cuisine, and I use it in my chilli oil and dan dan noodles. It has tongue-tingling and temporary numbing abilities, making it so addictive! Buy whole, toast, and crush in a pestle and mortar for best effect. I tend to buy the Bart brand.

Tahini
Tahini is a Middle Eastern condiment made from toasted ground sesame. It is served by itself or as a main ingredient in hummus, baba ghanoush and halva. It's a great ingredient in Asian food too; anywhere where peanut butter might be used, it gives a nutty depth and silky texture. It's also a brilliant non-dairy alternative to use in a creamy dressing. I like the Belazu or Al Nakhil brands.

Tajín Seasoning
A Mexican seasoning that is tangy from dried limes, salty and only barely spicy. It has a bright citrusy taste with a subtle chilli flavour – and it's great on both sweet and savoury foods.

Tamarind Paste
Tamarind is used in Asian cooking to add a tart yet sweet flavour. Made from a sour, dark, sticky fruit that grows in pods on a tamarind tree, you can buy tamarind concentrate or paste in the shops. Paste is usually blended whereas the concentrate has a treacle-like consistency and double the potency.

Thai Basil
Native to Southeast Asia, Thai basil has robust liquorice notes with sweet undertones. A beautiful herb added to curries and stir-fries towards the end of cooking to keep its fragrance. I love it fresh in my pomelo salad, and it's a quintessential flavour in pad krapow gai. The leaves are very delicate and won't last longer than a few days in the fridge. Available in most supermarkets.

Whole Spices
I always keep the following whole spices for infusing oils in a curry and crushing into a powder for intensity. They are my holy grail whole spices in their natural form: cinnamon sticks and bark, cloves, green and black cardamom pods, black peppercorns, cumin seeds, mustard seeds, fennel seeds, coriander seeds, bay leaves and whole dried chillies.

Za'atar
Every region in the Middle East has its own precious blend of za'atar. A spice mix bursting with earthy and exotic melodies of dried thyme, marjoram, sumac and sesame seeds, it's brilliant sprinkled over vegetables or mixed into marinades for a big flavour bomb. My favourite brands are Ren's Pantry and Zaytoun.

tablescaping & plating

Eating at a table is ceremonious for me, and my dining experiences bring the restaurant home. There is a trend of people wanting to stay home and dine in more, so with this in mind, transforming your ordinary dining space into a magical setting helps to create those memories and welcomes the sense of occasion. Sitting around the table with friends and family, sharing, talking, relaxing and eating is the joy of a dinner party in your own home.

And there's a new buzz word: tablescape! Your dinner table is the landscape for creating the atmosphere for your dinner party and elevating the experience. How many times have you picked a restaurant based on its beautiful decor? This is the same concept – making your guests feel special and relaxed.

Let your creativity and personality shine through as you create your own tablescape. There is no need to go shopping for expensive tableware – follow my simple tips for table styling overleaf.

plan

The type of dinner party will dictate the setting. If you are having sharing platters, for example, you might not want too much in the centre so you can place large plates down. If you have an outdoor setting, then maybe think candles inside a lantern and no flyaway napkins and tablecloths.

I like to plan my tablescapes around the seasons, but this doesn't mean buying different colours for each season. You can use seasonal fruits, for example, or flowers and foliage from your garden.

lay & layer

Tablecloths are the obvious answer to cover a table that doesn't look great in its raw state, and I would opt for a natural cotton or a versatile print. But personally, I can't be bothered to iron and wash a tablecloth, so I prefer to let the natural table peek through and instead use the plates and maybe some natural rattan placemats to create the sense of opulence.

You can now find very inexpensive table mats online or in the home section of supermarkets, which can be used time and time again. I have bought hessian rolls of fabric and cheesecloth fabric for times when I want a central focus, and buying fabric in this way is often cheaper than buying a product called 'table runner'.

Now use the concept of layering to lift your table setting to an indulgent level. I love cotton napkins in a natural colour or white; buy a set of 6 and reuse. The feeling of draping a napkin over your knees gives you that restaurant feel.

On each guest's tablemat, you can place a main plate down, sometimes referred to as the 'charger' plate. This can be a decorative plate if your guests aren't using it (in other words their plate of food will sit on top of this), equally it can be the plate they use if you are not plating up for them. Don't worry if they don't match; sometimes that's half the beauty. If you like, a side plate can be placed on top.

Next, a cotton napkin can either be draped over both plates, placed under the charger plate or put underneath the side plate in a waterfall fashion. You can also tie a mini brown luggage tag around the napkin with the guest's name, or a loose knot and insert a sprig of rosemary or a stick of cinnamon. If you decide to do printed menus, this can be placed on the plate, or a name tag can be written on a leaf or pebble. Many places online do laser-cut wooden name tags which serve as a keepsake. This is just an extra idea if you want to give your guests something memorable to take away (some might prefer a doggy bag for breakfast instead!).

plates & cutlery

Don't worry if your plates don't match – that's part of the charm of boho chic! Just make sure they're dishwasher safe (if you're lucky enough to have one). Nobody wants a pile of dishes to wash when there's a machine that can do it for you!

When it comes to plates, I usually go for a big one and a smaller side plate if needed. The number of plates and cutlery you need will depend on your menu. I prefer neutral plates like white or black, and then I add pops of colour with flowers and candles.

If you're using sharing platters, mix it up! Combine different colours, sizes and textures to keep things interesting. I like to use a mix of wooden boards, stainless steel, copper and printed porcelain.

As for cutlery, I try to keep a special set for those fancy occasions like Christmas or birthdays. But honestly, you can totally use your everyday set. All you really need is a knife, fork, dessert spoon and teaspoon. I have a gold and black set just because it adds a little something extra to my table. When setting the table, I place the knife and fork on either side of the plate, with both spoons in the centre above the plate.

Remember, there's no strict rule here, but a general guideline is to work from the outside in. If you have enough, you can add another set of knife and fork for the starter and main course to heighten that restaurant experience. That way, you won't need to wash cutlery in between courses. But if you don't have enough, just ask your guests to keep their cutlery between courses to save time and hassle.

So, relax and go with the flow! Set your table in a casual boho-chic style, mix things up, and enjoy the laid-back vibe of your gathering.

candles & flowers

Foliage and candles are non-negotiable; they add so much softness. I love tall, tapered dinner candles, short stubby church candles and tealights, too. These are inexpensive and colours can be changed to suit your theme. Flickering candlelight and the glow light up your guests' faces with warmth, and photographs look like they are taken during the golden hour.

You can now buy faux foliage like eucalyptus that can be laid in the middle of your table and candlesticks and small vases can be placed to hold flowers. You can also use screw-top jars, small milk bottles and even drinking glasses to hold flowers. Fresh flowers from the supermarket, like sturdy roses or geraniums, work well when mixed with faux foliage. Even spray gypsophila looks delicate, yet it's so cheap. In spring, daffodils bought a few days before the dinner party will bloom and bring instant sunshine to your table. If you are lucky enough to have one, pick flowers from your garden. Use herbs too – potted herbs like basil look pretty, fragrance the table, and again, are inexpensive and can be used in your cooking the following week.

Don't waste money on fragranced candles: let the aroma of the food and foliage perfume the table.

glasses

Sometimes we get caught up in the food and forget about the drinks. If you are making your guests cocktails, there is no need to set the table with too many glasses. As a rule, I always place water glasses and a water jug. This saves you getting up midway through a meal to get water. If drinking wine, set the table with wine glasses too, which will also give height to your tablescape. If you don't have stem glasses, that's okay, as wine can also be drunk out of nice tumblers.

height

As well as colour, texture and practicality, it's very important to consider height when creating your tablescape. You don't want faces blocked by over-intruding tall vases of flowers, and I prefer to add height with candlesticks and tapered candles instead. Equally ensure low decor like tealights and stubby candles are included, and even the water bottle and glasses will add interesting height.

finishing touches

Don't forget music! It adds atmosphere to the dinner-party experience. I like to pick something quite relaxing so guests don't rush their food. The tempo naturally increases as the dinner party progresses and the wine decreases!

I like to add the finishing touches of name tags on the table, mixing people up to encourage new conversations. No need to keep it formal, and I prefer natural tones like leaves or stones. Wine corks or old postcards also set a great vibe. If you have time and want to create the excitement of anticipation, you could write the menu out on a blackboard or just some brown paper and put it into a frame. For my dinner parties that have several courses, I tend to do individual menus that are typed out and placed on every placemat. Although this is a little time consuming, it's worth the effort if you do want to go the extra mile. There are many free templates online to help you put this together.

tablescape hire

There are also several companies who will now send you a tablescape in a box if you don't have the storage space or want someone to do the design for you. This is an expensive option, but worth considering if you'd like to learn how to put together a professional-looking tablescape with guidance.

my top 5 plating tricks

This might sound like a cliché, but like most clichés it's true: your first bite is with the eye. Your taste buds predict on appearance how much they will enjoy the dish. Presentation is so important, but it needn't be fussy or complicated. Keep these tips in mind when plating your food at your next dinner party, or even when you plate yourself dinner – take pride in your plate!

1. visualize

When I create a dish I try to imagine what it will look like in my head. I first think about the elements, the colours and what background it will need to make the food 'pop' – a plate or a bowl, dark or light. I often draw out where everything will go and build on it from there. I don't want the crockery to distract from the food, so if the food is colourful, the plate needs to be muted.

If it's canapés or sharing plates, I will seek out everything I own, from bamboo baskets to wooden chopping boards or slates to present everything in a different way.

2. keep it simple

Focus on one main ingredient and centre everything else around it. Don't complicate the plate with unnecessary garnish or sauces. Focus on the main element being cooked well, and let the empty areas of the plate make the main element stand out. Choose the right plates and bowls to go with the theme of the food. Crockery makes a huge difference to how the presentation works: think colour, size, texture and also practicality.

3. express yourself

Let your personality shine on the plate. Play with colours, shapes and textures. However, the presentation shouldn't overwhelm the flavour. Try not to get trapped in the style-over-substance chaos.

4. garnish

An easy way to elevate your dishes to restaurant standard is by using micro cress, edible flowers and flavoured powders. But the rule of thumb is to only use something if it enhances the flavour.

I love the delicate look of coriander (cilantro) cress on dumplings and curries. Pea tendrils have such a good structure to add height and animation. Edible flowers add flavour and colour. I like to pick individual petals to decorate my dish rather than using the whole flower, which I find overpowering. Freeze-dried powders such as beetroot (beet) or spinach, dusted onto the plates, give an artistic look to complement the ingredients on the plate. They are now widely available online.

I also love using crackers and tuiles for texture, height and interesting presentation. Rice paper and noodles are a great ingredient when deep-fried to add crunch and drama to a dish.

5. trends

As with fashion, food has trends, and plating also goes through trends. There are foams and purées, drizzles and smears, and food plating will change, but ultimately your influence should be your surroundings, personality and the ingredients. The trend is currently moving away from traditional plated food and the emphasis is on sharing platters and small plates. Use the tips above to inspire you to make beautiful yet unfussy plates. Enjoy the process of plating up.

menu plans

Follow these menu plans to get the best out of ingredients at their seasonal best and discover a stress-free way to host for 2–12. Choose any of the dishes for two- or three-course meals and mix it up for sharing plates. For larger numbers, choose a few starters and complementary mains if you want to really show off!

spring

Starters
Bombay Crab Crumpets 41
Japanese Asparagus Fritti 24
Lamb Gyoza-Samosa 31

Mains
Coconut Saag Paneer with Peas 79
Mombasa Prawn Masala 88
Gochujang Lamb Chops with Summery Noodle
   Slaw 99

Dessert
Banoffee Pie Dumplings 142
Piña Colada Tarte Tatin 149
Brown Butter Madeleines & Pomegranate Glaze 154

summer

Starters
Roasted Harissa Carrots with Whipped Feta
   & Crispy Chickpeas 98
Grilled Lemon Courgettes with Cardamom
   Labneh 119
Tajín Watermelon & Halloumi 112

Mains
Aubergine Tarte Tatin 46
Thai Sea Bass Parcels with Coconut Rice
   & Asian Slaw 48
Sri Lankan Chicken Masala Traybake 90

Dessert
Strawberry & Lemongrass Posset 164
Grilled Amaretto Peaches with Whipped Amaretti
   Mascarpone 156
Papaya Pavlova 147

autumn

Starters
Roast Beetroot with Whipped Goat's Cheese
   & Thai Pesto 110
Nduja Scallops with Silky Corn & Nori 67
Fig, Mozzarella & Aleppo Cashews 103

Mains
Keralan Monkfish & Clams with Samphire
   Pakoras 48
Delica Pumpkin Laksa 92
Langkawi Chicken Rendang 87

Dessert
Kataifi Pistachio Cheesecake with Berries 158
Cardamom & Chocolate Orange Tea Cups 150
Cheat's Cappuccino Brioche with Gelato 153

winter

Starters
Blood Orange & Za'atar Burrata with Hazelnuts 106
Crispy Potato Maru Bhajia 42
Malaysian Jackfruit Coconut Curry Puffs 37

Mains
Goan Salmon Curry 76
Whole Cauliflower Shawarma with Pistachio
   Yogurt 51
Miso Mushroom & Lentil Lasagne 117

Dessert
Coconut Lime Leaf Pannacotta with Passionfruit
   & Sesame Honeycomb 144
Matcha Ice Cream 163
Tahini & Chocolate Chunk Cookies 148

2–4 guests

Starters (or pick 2–3 for sharing plates)
Nori Tostadas with Tajín 18
Crispy Tofu Pancakes 25
Edamame & Truffle Gyoza 32
Vietnamese Street Fries 96
Blood Orange & Za'atar Burrata with Hazelnuts 106
Nduja Scallops with Silky Corn & Nori 67
Bombay Crab Crumpets 41
Grilled Lemon Courgettes with Labneh 119

Mains
Butter Chicken Sphere 60
Keralan Monkfish & Clams with Samphire Pakoras 48
Ebi Katsu Curry 52
Sri Lankan Chicken Masala Traybake 90
Aubergine Tarte Tatin 46
Goan Salmon Curry 76
Whole Cauliflower Shawarma with Pistachio Yogurt 51
English Breakfast Parathas 64
Hariyali Chicken Biriyani Traybake 58
Alleppey Houseboat Mushroom Curry 85

Dessert
Banoffee Pie Dumplings 142
Kataifi Pistachio Cheesecake with Berries 158
Papaya Pavlova 147

4–8 guests

Starters (or pick 3–5 for sharing plates)
Sea Bass Roti Tacos 22
Lamb Gyoza-Samosa 31
Spicy Teriyaki Blistered Padrón & Edamame 34
Crispy Sambal Chicken Wings 102
Creamiest Hummus Ever 129
Vietnamese Street Fries 96
Korean Chicken Bao Buns 55
Crispy Herb & Silken Chilli Tofu 109

Mains
Langkawi Chicken Rendang 87
Gochujang Rigatoni 124
Asian Hispi Cabbage with Tahini Butter Beans & Chilli Oil 104

Sri Lankan Chicken Masala Traybake 90
Dan Dan Noodles with Cucumber 54
Thai Sea Bass Parcels with Coconut Rice & Asian Slaw 63
Ganesh's Butter Chicken 82
Roasted Harissa Carrots with Whipped Feta & Crispy Chickpeas 98
Lamb Kofta Masala 93
Coconut Saag Paneer with Peas 79

Dessert
Grilled Amaretto Peaches with Whipped Amaretti Mascarpone 156
Coconut Lime Leaf Pannacotta with Passionfruit & Sesame Honeycomb 144
Brown Butter Madeleines & Pomegranate Glaze 154

8–12 guests

Starters (or pick 3–5 for sharing plates)
Chilli Paneer Dumplings 28
Bombay Beetroot Bubble 21
Malaysian Jackfruit Coconut Curry Puffs 37
Sesame Halloumi with Chilli Honey 43
Red Thai Arancini 16
Sweet Potato & Cumin Wontons 36
Cheat's Turkish Manti 126
Thai Pomelo Salad 113

Mains
Harissa Salmon with Rocket Chimichurri & Za'atar Potatoes 114
Miso Mushroom & Lentil Lasagne 117
Thai Basil Chicken 74
Red Thai Daal with Coconut Sambal 72
10-Minute Sticky Chinese Chicken 138
Gochujang Lamb Chops with Summery Noodle Slaw 99
Sri Lankan Chicken Masala Traybake 90
Roast Beetroot with Whipped Goat's Cheese & Thai Pesto 110
10-Minute Tantanmen Ramen 131
Aubergine Tarte Tatin 46

Dessert
Cheat's Cappuccino Brioche with Gelato 153
Strawberry & Lemongrass Posset 164
Cardamom & Chocolate Orange Tea Cups 150

index

acknowledgements – the thank yous

It definitely takes a small village to build a book. The sheer love and dedication of all these individuals have contributed to the precious pages that I SHARE with you today.

Friends and Family

Sachin – not only my husband, but my number 1 fan. Without your constant harassment and persistence for 10 years to fill out the application form for MasterChef, I would never have changed the course of my life: all your encouragement, guidance and cheerleading. Only you recognised that my food should be shared, and for that, I am eternally grateful. Thank you for making me discover my purpose. Thank you for this beautiful life adventure we SHARE together.

Sai & Druv – my hungry boys and my biggest critics. Thank you for being such foodies, for being so brutally honest about my dishes and injecting all the laughter into the kitchen. Without Alexa blaring out loud music while you kick a football around me as I try to roll out chapatis, my world wouldn't be complete – you create the fun chaos!

Mum & Dad – it goes without saying that Mum you have had the biggest impact in my appreciation for cooking, food and hosting. All the joy you had when inviting people to your legendary dinner parties has certainly rubbed off on me. You would force me to stay in the kitchen, and all those skills you taught me have helped share my love of hosting as a career. Dad – thank you for taking me to the library every Monday since the age of 5 to spend hours engrossed in books. Appreciating the art of words has helped me write this book, and also thank you for your advice on getting business savvy. Investing 17 years in the corporate world has benefited me massively to set up my own business.

My In-laws – thank you for teaching me new dishes in the kitchen from Nairobi and Mombasa. Thank you for always being there to babysit and drop round food when I've had events to attend.

My little sisters, Avni & Hina – asking me constantly for recipes and what to cook when you have people coming round has been my best training course! Thanks for being my testing crew and always taking leftovers – I would like all my tupperware back at some point please! Your cheerleading on my journey and endless support has meant everything to me.

Joe Wicks – I will never forget the day you asked to speak to the chef at the Soccer Aid Gala in London 2019 where I designed the menu you enjoyed. Apart from MasterChef, meeting you that evening changed my life. You have been my biggest supporter, shouting about me on your Instagram page. At the many dinner parties I have cooked for you and Rosie, you said – why don't you write a book? I replied I can't do that, I wouldn't know where to start? Then you introduced me to your agent Bev James and the idea of this book was born. I'm eternally grateful to you for believing in me even before I had the confidence to do so myself. I've loved your journey and seeing your family grow. I am thrilled to SHARE my journey with you.

John Terry – thank you for your kindness and warmth every time I come into your home, and for helping me grow my business and inspiring me to write this book. I adore cooking for you, Toni and your friends. It's been a joy seeing the twins grow up, I'm so glad they like curry too!

Stephen Miron – 'I have eaten around the world, and your food is world class'. I was blown away by your comment. Thank you for booking me regularly for your dinner parties, thank you for supporting this book and thank you for the music, and inviting me and my family to SHARE the magic of the Capital Summertime and Jingle Bell Ball. I treasure the moments I spend with you and the family.

The Book Family

Sophie Allen – our constant laughing has kept me going through this lonely process of book writing. Your encouragement and excitement about my recipes and your vision for this book has been invaluable. You have truly helped me create something more beautiful than I imagined. We still have a long list of restaurants to visit and SHARE more funny stories together. You are a remarkable talent, thank you for always holding my hand.

Gemma Hayden – your vision and creativity has really brought SHARE to life. Thank you for capturing the atmosphere of hosting with the colours, textures and mood. Your attention to detail is exquisite.

Faye Wears – it really helps when you have identical taste! Thanks for selecting the most perfect crockery, linens, candlesticks and all the props – can you be my personal shopper for life? You know exactly what I love!

Amy Stephenson – how we clicked instantly and belly laughed, like long lost friends! Every shoot with you was effortless, you made my dishes sing on the plate. It was a bonus you loved my food and I was delighted there were doggy bags for Aaron too! Learnt so much from you, you have such a creative eye, thanks for putting up with my 'faff'!

Nassima Rothacker – you are a beautiful ball of spiritual energy. I felt so calm and safe in your hands – your natural aura for just taking the most stunning photos effortlessly. Thank you for making every shoot day so easy, with your delicious soothing teas and mood-boosting oils. Your talent is so obvious, I felt very lucky to have my book shot by you. Forever grateful.

Bev James – thank you for having faith in me to do this book. I remember at our first meeting when I said I would like to showcase my food from my travels, you immediately said but dinner parties are your forte, we should do a dinner party cookbook! Thank you for your direction, belief and encouragement always. This book wouldn't have been possible without your team and fantastic literary agents.

Aoife & Tom – always there when I felt like I was having a wobble. It's been a long lonely road writing this book, but you were always there on the phone and zooms to pick me up and keep me going. Thank you for keeping my excitement levels constantly high!

John & Gregg – thank you both for giving me the opportunity to showcase my food on BBC's MasterChef. This experience totally changed the course of my life and turned my passion into a job. Without the platform you have both created it would have taken me years to break into the food industry. Thank you for helping me discover my true calling. Forever grateful for where this journey first started.

Jaimini & Jamie – without my J&J dream team none of my dinner parties would have been possible and this book wouldn't exist. From the days of the cafe, to all the private dinners we host together, I couldn't do this alone. You both have full-time jobs and give up your Saturdays selflessly to help me, you are like my family. We create dinner party memories for others to cherish but equally I treasure how our friendship has flourished and every private dining together is utter joy with a selfie to prove it! I have loved sharing this journey with you both, thanks for being there from day one.

My Followers – this book is for you. It has been inspired by all of you who have followed my journey since MasterChef and especially over the pandemic. I owe you all my thanks and more. The regular requests for recipes I cook at my events are now in your hands. The love and support from all of you, knowing that you wanted my recipes in print has made this possible. I hope it becomes your saving grace when you have people coming round, or when you just want to cook your family/friends something nice on the weekend. It's my absolute joy to SHARE these recipes with you, for moments you can SHARE with others.

about the author

Nisha Parmar rose to culinary fame on BBC's MasterChef UK in 2018, where she was celebrated for her signature presentation style, authentic family recipes, and travel-inspired Asian cuisine.

A few years on, Nisha has transformed her lifelong passion for homemade food into a successful cooking career after quitting her job as a Private Banker in the City after 17 years. A mother of two boys, Nisha is a full time private chef, restaurant consultant, supper club host and a content creator for prestigious food brands.

Following her success with hosting dinner parties, Nisha has become one of the most popular names in celebrity dining experiences. Her signature dishes have attracted a range of A-lister clients such as Joe Wicks, Peter Jones (Dragon's Den) and Alesha Dixon (BGT) to premier footballers including John Terry and UK pop icons Ronan Keating and Ellie Goulding.

Nisha has showcased her menus in grand venues and special events, including The Unicef Soccer Aid Gala at The Science Museum in London and in St Paul's Cathedral for a charity Christmas banquet.

The COVID-19 pandemic posed challenges to many, but Nisha's resilience and creativity shone through. She responded by filming her lunch and dinner, creating over 100 recipe videos to help people cook nutritious meals at home with some restaurant favouites as people missed going out to eat.

This initiative not only showcased her culinary expertise but also created a supportive community of fans. Nisha's relatability as a mother, risk-taker and trailblasing British South Asian female has resonated deeply with her audience, endearing her to people who admire her not only for her cooking but also for her ability to connect on a personal level.

Nisha's background as a British South Asian with roots in both Kenya and India adds an extra layer of richness to her culinary identity. Her ability to blend and evolve traditional Indian flavours with her unique experiences and diverse heritage demonstrates the evolution of Indian/Asian cuisine.